Upstream
on the
Mataura

Dougal Rillstone caught his first trout in the Mataura River in 1953, and has fished it almost every year since. He was born close to the river, and continues to own a fishing cottage 10 minutes from the Mataura. In 1998 he was individual champion at the Oceania Fly Fishing Championships, held in the Snowy Mountains, Australia. He has contributed to high-end magazines *Gray's Sporting Journal* in the United States, and *FlyLife* in Australia.

For Dylan, Elliot, George and Maeve.

Upstream
on the
Mataura

A Fly Fisher's Journey to Source

Dougal Rillstone

MARY EGAN
PUBLISHING

Extract from *Time on the Waters* reproduced with the permission
of Kevin Ireland.

Extract from *The movie may be slightly different* reproduced with the
permission of Vincent O'Sullivan.

'Fortune Creek' was first published in *Gray's Sporting Journal*, USA.

'Why I Fish' was first published in *FlyLife*, Australia.

Published by Mary Egan Publishing
www.maryegan.co.nz

This edition published 2020

© Dougal Rillstone 2020

The right of Dougal Rillstone to be identified
as the author of this work in terms of section 96 of the
Copyright Act 1994 is hereby asserted.

Designed, typeset and produced by Mary Egan Publishing
Cover designed by Anna Egan-Reid
Cover photographs © Andrew Harding
NZ Topo Map c/- LINZ © Crown Copyright Reserved
Printed in China

ISBN 978-0-473-51307-8

CONTENTS

PART TWO

The river was our pool. *L–R:* Dougal, cousin Suzanne, Bruce,
Dad holding brother John.

PREFACE

We remember our first paths — with our unsureness.
BRUCE CHATWIN

When I turned sixty-five, Mum gave me a new copy of *Scuffy the Tugboat*, a book she and Dad read to me almost as far back as I can remember. I loved the story of the tugboat heading off downstream from the green uplands into the ever-growing river where Scuffy encountered things of wonder and danger, before ending his journey back where he started — in the bathtub with the little boy, watched over by his father with a yellow polka-dot bow-tie. The story is, of course, a metaphor for life but that was lost on me when I was three or four. What it left me with was a sense of the excitement and danger involved in long river journeys. Seeing the book again ignited my interest to go on my own long journey beside the river I loved. It would be my tribute to the river, and I sensed that if I delayed doing it, I might not be able to.

A couple of years before Mum gave me the book I had started to write about my experiences as a fly fisher. Many of the stories were centred on the Mataura, because it has been the river of my life. Eventually I decided to combine my story of walking the Mataura with other stories centred on the river and its tributaries. The stories are as much about friends and family as they are about the river and trout. They don't offer detailed descriptions of how to catch trout, but I hope the way I have fished these rivers and streams shines through in the stories. Some of them are cautionary tales about the decline of some of my once-favourite places, because it would be dishonest not to face up to what's going on with our rivers. I hope the stories convey the love I feel for the Mataura and its tributaries, and the excitement that grips me still when chasing trout with a fly rod, sixty-five years after my heart was captured by a fish.

My first memory involves a trout, and the Mataura River. On a summer afternoon in 1953, just south of Gore, I caught my first trout. I had recently turned four, and the impact of the fish was so powerful the memory of the afternoon hasn't left me. The tentative nodding of the rod tip as the fish nibbled the worm, my rush to grab the bending rod, the pulse of the fish felt through my arms, and the flood of excitement it unleashed is with me still. As is the fish lying beside me on the gravel, its deep, speckled sides and dark eyes — so soft to the touch. My connection with the Mataura started earlier, though, in the first days of my life.

Late in the summer of 1949 I was born a long stone's throw from the river that splits the town of Gore in two. Mum recently told me about the eight weeks she spent in Gore hospital towards the end of her pregnancy with me. By the time I was born, she said, she had despaired she might never make it home, so when Dad drove the three of us over the Gore bridge she insisted he stop — on River Terrace, beside the Mataura, as it happened — where she cried with relief at finally leaving the hospital. As a premature baby in a back-seat cot I wouldn't have been aware of much, so I can't lay claim to hearing the sound of the river as it swished past. I am, though, pleased that my first journey had me crossing the Mataura River, and for a short time being parked beside it — albeit with Mum crying in the front seat. Since hearing the story I've sometimes wondered if the river magically touched my heart that February afternoon.

I have a record of one of the first encounters I had with the river. It's a photograph taken by Mum in the summer of 1950–51. I'm sitting chest-deep in the river near the northern outskirts of Gore at a place I later knew as the Bend. Dad is pictured standing over me, hands on knees, looking down on my bonneted head, while the Mataura flows around us. He looks as if he was watching out for me, to be sure I wasn't swept off by the current, but I see more in his pose — a look of love, perhaps, or pride, as he looked down on his first child. Our house in Wentworth Street was three blocks to the east, and my grandparents lived between our place and the river, on the edge of farmland, a couple of paddocks from the flood-bank. Until I left for university when I was seventeen, this part of East Gore, bounded by the Mataura and the Waikaka Stream, was my world.

Through the fifties the river was our pool. We didn't own a car to take us into town, even if another pool had existed, so on those few warm nights of the southern summer we walked or biked to the river to swim. One night in particular remains with me. I was swimming with Dad. Perhaps twenty people swam or watched from the bank that windless evening. I stood chest-deep in a long pool, facing downstream looking into the fading light, while all around us rings left by rising trout rippled outwards, colliding with each other on the otherwise smooth surface. It was what I imagine local anglers called 'the mad Mataura rise', and it left me mesmerised.

We did most of our swimming at the Bend, where the river dropped off a curving ripple into a deep willow-lined hole. I would watch Dad swinging from a rope into the pool, and felt both entranced and frightened by the dark, swirling water. Later I swung off the same rope and tasted the water as I kicked to the surface through a swirl of bubbles, before paddling to the bank and clinging to willow roots while my friends flew through the air above me — before they too hit the water.

I often bought a parcel of oysters and chips for one shilling and sixpence on my way home from the Saturday matinee movie. I ate them while I dawdled over the bridge watching trout lurking behind almost every obstruction or indentation in the riverbed. Mostly they held their position in the flow, but once in a while they dashed sideways, or upwards to take something from the surface. I simply loved watching them — these wild creatures, being embedded in my imagination. I wasn't aware of it at the time, but it was the best possible education into the habits of trout. By the time I went to high school I was as tethered to the Mataura by my early experiences as I imagine a salmon is to its natal place.

While my connection with the Mataura was formed during my childhood, it has been fishing — fly-fishing in particular — that's kept me close to the river over the decades. Not only has it been my excuse to spend over 1500 days on the Mataura and its tributaries, but the intensity of the looking that's integral to being a fly fisher has given me an understanding and appreciation of the river that otherwise would be impossible.

Michael McCarthy, when writing about the chalk streams of southern England in *The Moth Snowstorm*, said they were largely unappreciated outside the culture of angling:

> [In] fly fishing and its literature, these rivers were given their due, but beyond that, they might have been on the moon. Poets did not sing them. Painters did not paint them. Writers did not write about them, even nature writers who wrote about many aspects of the countryside, unless they happened to be fishermen too . . . [They]

seemed, and still seem to have no place in the national consciousness.

What he said is true of the Mataura. It is a catchment of over 5400 square kilometres, and the only poem I could find that features a river in the system was by my old friend Brian Turner who, almost forty years ago, in his collection *Bones* dedicated a poem to me called 'October on the Otamita'.

Some streams have attracted the attention of writers. Dylan Thomas called the valley his beloved Aaron flowed through the most beautiful in the world, and Seamus Heaney who lived beside the Moyola wrote lovingly of it — but the Mataura has mostly been ignored by writers. Perhaps the people who settled near it were too busy establishing their existence in what probably felt like alien land to be seduced by the aesthetics of the place.

I find poetry, though, in the names of the rivers and streams that for at least 12,000 years have snaked their way across the landscape of the place we now call Southland. Like the slow-moving tectonic plates and glaciers before them, they have shaped the landscape. They are, in the rough order they join the Mataura: Roberts Creek, Bright Water, Eyre Creek, Parawa Stream, Nokomai River, Tomogalak Stream, Waikaia River, Dome Burn, Argyle Burn, Wendon Stream, Fortune Creek, Otamita Stream, Waimea Stream, Waikaka Stream, Mimihau Stream, Venlaw Stream, Mokoreta River, Redan Stream.

There are others, often without name, that connect with the Mataura. Some show as blue lines on my topographical maps, and some are unmarked, but all are important to the living river.

There is a human scale to the Mataura and its tributaries. Unless in high flood when they can invoke fear, they are intimate, and mostly able to be waded and crossed with ease. Some start their lives from bogs and tarns in the high snow tussock, some seep from mountainous scree slopes, and others emerge from deep aquifers. Some flow through bush-clad valleys, some through land swathed in tussock, and others through avenues of willows and beside grassy banks. The music they make matches the geography of their path. In the high country their boisterous tumble can be so raucous as to drown out the sound of the birds and wind, while on the plains they mostly glide through the land, leaving not much more than a murmur as a record of their passing. They finish their journey as one river, whispering through the last of the land — in the broad quietness that Bertrand Russell thought a metaphor for the later stages of our lives — before reaching the Southern Ocean where they mingle with water from all the rivers that have ever flowed.

The first trout released into the catchment went into the Otamita in 1869. That release was followed by others in the Otamita in 1871 and 1872. The trout thrived, and a catch of 120 trout averaging over four pounds was recorded from the Otamita before 1889. There are no records of releases of trout into the Mataura since the early 1950s. For over seventy years the river has been a self-sustaining fishery for brown trout. *The Mataura Trout Fishery* (Witherow and Scott, 1984) reported that in the 1970s around 20,000 trout were taken annually from the Mataura. They showed that the river had a large population of fast-growing, good-sized brown trout, and I believe the same is largely true today. According to the *NIWA National Angling Survey 2014–15*, the angling effort on the Mataura has dropped in recent years, from around 65,000 angling days in 1994–95 to around 36,000 today. It is a trend my angling friends don't believe, instead perceiving more anglers than ever competing for the best places on the river. They may be right, but anglers have made such claims for centuries. Back in 1598 Thomas Bastard wrote that 'fishes decrease, and fishers multiply'. What is true is that a higher proportion of those who fish the river do so above Gore than was the case earlier, and visitors from outside the region in particular favour the upper river.

Expert angler diary surveys have shown that skilled anglers catch an average of a trout an hour on the Mataura, while others must toil for five hours for each fish. Mere statistics, though, don't do the river justice as a trout fishery. All that needs to be said about the fishery is that there are more than enough large wild trout in the rivers and streams that form the Mataura, and that many of them will take a carefully presented fly. I believe it to be one of the great brown trout fisheries left on the planet.

Writing about my walk and the stories connecting me to the river has ignited in me an interest in my earliest ancestors in the area. The Stanfords and Patersons settled a little west of the Mataura, in Lumsden, in the first decade or so of the Scots, English and Irish reaching the valley. My grandmother, Bella Rillstone (née Paterson) was born there in 1883. She died a year before I was born, leaving untold the stories she might have been able to tell me of the river and her experiences of crossing it on horse and cart.

When I caught my first trout back in 1953, I had no idea where the rush of excitement I felt would take me. Certainly, there was no expectation that over time I would be drawn into an ever-deeper connection with the river. Nor that I would feel joy at seeing it at its best, running clear over a bottom rich with insect life, or the pain I would feel while watching the tussock protecting parts of its catchment lacerated in the name of increased agricultural production.

In 1953 I couldn't have imagined that my most enduring friendships would form around a love of the river and the trout that live in it, nor that the river would hold us together even as our views about many of the things that matter have veered off in different directions. Without the Mataura, and the time we have spent together, walking the river searching for trout, these friendships wouldn't have begun, let alone survived, and my life would have been diminished as a consequence.

And, perhaps most important, I couldn't have foreseen back

in 1953 that the time I spent on the river, looking into the water, would gradually allow me to see beyond the river, into myself. It has given me insight into where I stand in the scheme of things, about what matters, and about what is of little consequence. For all of this, I am deeply grateful.

PART ONE

WALKING UPSTREAM ON
THE MATAURA

I started thinking about walking the length of Southland's 190-kilometre Mataura River sometime in 2015. At first it wasn't much more than an idle dream, but it eventually crystallised into something I couldn't resist. For a few years I had wished that someone who had loved the river had written about it, say, in the early part of the last century, leaving a record of what the river was like then and what it meant to the people who cared about the Mataura.

It has taken me decades to understand just how extraordinary the Mataura is as a brown trout fishery. At the start I was perhaps too absorbed in the fishing to judge it against the other great trout rivers on the planet. While I'm sure others did understand its place in the pantheon of brown trout fisheries, no one it seems had attempted to make the case for the Mataura in writing.

It wasn't until the 1980s, when I began to devour as much good angling literature as I could find, that I was able to put the Mataura into a wider perspective. The fly-fishing I was enjoying then was as good or better than that I read about in the best stories of the great rivers and streams of the United States, England, Ireland and Scotland, which for me were the homes of the sport I loved. And those experiences from people like Joe Brooks, Negley Farson, Charles Fox, Vincent Marinaro, Robert Traver, G. E. M. Skues, John Waller Hills and Frank Sawyer mostly referred to an earlier golden era.

A decade or so later I visited a few of the fabled US streams I had read of, and while I appreciated the sense of angling history they held, it was clear to me that, for many, their time of being great fisheries for wild trout had passed.

There were other factors involved in my decision to walk the length of the river. Something about the physical challenge and the adventure involved appealed — a vanity perhaps — as I entered the second half of my seventh decade, when there is a temptation to consider those things best left to the young. There was, therefore, a certain irony in my inability to make the trip in the summer of 2016 due to persistent swelling and pain in one of my Achilles tendons. When my tendon eventually healed during the winter of 2016, I began to build my walking fitness for the journey by getting out of bed while it was still dark and heading off on hour-long walks around Dunedin's hill suburbs with my wife, Sue. I was used to walking long distances while fishing, but the uncertainty I felt was related to how well my body would cope with covering rough ground for a couple of weeks.

The US writer and fly fisher Thomas McGuane made some comments about our knowledge of rivers that also influenced my walk. He said that we can only truly know one river in our lives, and even then just one part of that river in an intimate way. At this more reflective stage of my life I accept McGuane's comments to be true. Over the years I have known different sections of the river with the intimacy that I believe he meant: first as a boy when I knew the river half a day's bike ride either side of Gore; and in the later stages of my life I have grown to understand the essence of the Mataura and its tributaries from Otama to the Nokomai Gorge. I hoped the walk would help me tie these disparate intimacies together, and leave me with a deeper sense of the whole river.

Because I held a romantic notion that I would spend most nights camped beside the Mataura, the walk proved to be a good excuse to upgrade my camping gear. I bought a one-person Big Agnes tent that weighed less than a kilogram; a feather-light pack; a beautifully engineered lightweight gas cooker; an emergency locator beacon; and a power pack for my cellphone. In the spring I bought the series of Land Information New Zealand's Topo50 maps that covered the length of the river, and began the process of measuring and planning the route. My initial calculations were based on being able to cover thirty kilometres each day. That didn't feel too daunting a task based on the extent of river I sometimes covered on a day's fishing, particularly as the hours of daylight would be long. I figured that walking four hours in the morning and another four in the afternoon would have me easily covering thirty kilometres, and leave me an hour or two to fish, eat and reflect. The route I measured along the river looked to be about 250 kilometres, which meant it should be completed in around nine days. I double-checked the route using Google Earth, which allowed me to fly along the path I thought I would take and decide where the river might be crossed in those sections that I wasn't familiar with.

I also visited the Hocken Collections at the University of Otago library in Dunedin, looking out as much written material as I could find on some of the places I would pass through, as well as observations from some of the early European settlers in the Mataura Valley. It was a deeply fulfilling experience, because it left me with a picture of what the valley looked like in the 1850s when the first English and Scots settlers left the coast to explore the area. Reports of the first encounters with the Māori who occupied the coastal area and were seasonally active near Tuturau and the Mataura Falls were also helpful in lifting my understanding of what the river meant to them.

For a time I considered the direction I should take. My initial inclination was to start as high in the headwaters as I could manage, and walk with the flow to the Southern Ocean. It felt like the natural course to take, but over the years I have always preferred journeys that took me towards the highlands. I feared that after leaving the pristine start of the Mataura in the mountains, it would be downhill in more ways than one as I headed to the coast. Eventually I settled to start at the ocean and, like Benjamin Button, walk towards the birthplace of the river.

In the couple of years I was thinking about the walk I read a number of fine books on nature writing. Earlier I had read Annie Dillard, and Aldo Leopold's *A Sand County Almanac*, and while I prepared for the walk I read Robert Macfarlane's *The Old Ways* and *The Wild Places*, the Scottish Modernist writer Nan Shepherd's *The Living Mountain*, and the late Roger Deakin's *Waterlog: a swimmer's journey through Britain*. They set a dauntingly high standard, but inspired me to capture my experiences on the river in prose.

A month before I was due to start walking, I sent an email to Steve Lovemore, a friend from Cape Town, in which I outlined my route and included some map references so he could get a sense of the challenge. He has the spirit and experience of an adventurer, so I hoped to benefit from his thoughtful insights. His advice was clear: I was planning to cover too much ground each day — and because of that I wasn't allowing enough time to 'rest under a willow and absorb the experience'. Take a book with you, he said. He prescribed *As I Walked Out One Midsummer Morning* by Laurie Lee: it would be the perfect accompaniment for such a walk, he said.

It didn't take me long to accept that he was right. In my

desire to limit the time I was going to be away from Sue and home I had set targets that might have defeated the purpose of doing such a walk — turning it into a slog, rather than the reflective celebration of the river I hoped for. I adjusted my plans accordingly so that my daily target was reduced to about twenty kilometres, which pushed the expected duration of the walk out to twelve to fourteen days.

A couple of weeks out from the start I decided on the food I would need and purchased a quantity of dried food, nuts, cereals, high-energy protein bars and ground coffee. Instead of following my usual course at the supermarket of trying to limit the energy content of the things I buy, I went all out, looking for the maximum calories relative to the weight involved. I didn't, however, go as far as the Arctic explorer I had met in the United States a few years earlier. He told me he needed over five thousand calories a day for his solo sled trip to the Pole and back — and that the only way he could get them was in the form of butter, of which he chewed one and a half blocks a day.

A week before I was due to start the walk I clambered into my Cessna and flew towards Fortrose under a low grey ceiling to check out the best route along the lower river. A motor boat towed a waterskier over the wind-torn surface as I banked over the estuary. Even from a few hundred feet it was obvious that the swampy true left bank of the river would take ages to cross. I pulled the plane into another tight turn, flew low over the scores of whitebaiters' huts before heading down the rolling dunes of the sandspit that holds the Southern Ocean from over-running the estuary. The last few kilometres were deserted, with just the outline of an old four-wheel-drive track the only sign of recent human activity. It looked like the perfect place to start.

***

I became distracted and edgy in the days before the trip, and the night before I headed south with Sue and our two dogs my sleep was disturbed by nightmares, as though every old insecurity in my soul had surfaced to let me know what they thought of my journey. In the pre-dawn gloom, I lay wondering why I was making the trip. The earlier feelings of excitement had been replaced by a fear of the unknown, and a recognition of how lonely I would likely feel spending so many days mostly by myself. By the time we left Dunedin a solid headache pulsed behind my eyes, and my mind was so cluttered with doubt that I forgot to fill the car with fuel on the way south, saving the day with a stop at a pump in Edendale — the last before the coast.

'You lived here long?' I asked the woman at the country-style petrol station.

'We get away a bit, my husband and me, in our van — but yes, been here all my life,' she said with a rueful smile.

I looked towards the south coast and the piled clouds being driven hard by a westerly gale. 'Not much of a day. I'm planning to walk up the Mataura. Fished it most of my life,' I said, as though trying to explain what I was doing in the south.

'Summer hasn't started here yet,' she said. 'Spring was okay, but it's blown ever since. Hope it picks up for you, but the forecast is lousy.'

FORTROSE AND TOETOES BAY

We drove to Fortrose through a rolling green landscape of dairy and sheep farms, and dark shelter belts cowering eastwards away from the salty gales that charge off the Southern Ocean at Toetoes Bay. I had hoped to find someone at Fortrose with a boat able to take me across the narrow channel that separated the town from the start of my walk at the end of the sandspit, just half a kilometre away. What I guessed were a father and two daughters struggled to launch a blow-up dingy beyond the waves that the westerly wind pushed down the estuary while an anxious mother watched from a distance, but that wasn't the ride I had in mind. It was the only boat we saw.

Fortrose used to have a bank, school and port: in the 1830s it was the base for a major whaling station. For several centuries earlier Māori had gathered to catch fish and birds at this place where the Mataura River enters the ocean. The town's reason for being diminished over a hundred years ago when the whales had been hunted close to extinction, and the need for the port was ended by a rail link from Invercargill. It hangs on now on the edge of this empty coast, sustained by a summer flurry of tourists visiting the Catlins.

On the headland that is the last land on the eastern side of the Mataura, the wind driving off the ocean was so powerful we had to heave open the car doors and escape before they slammed shut. We stood on tussock laid low and desiccated not by a lack of rain but by the salt spray and gales that flayed the hard rock cliffs and the rolling land beyond. I stood looking at the place where the early ebb of the tide allowed the fresh water of the Mataura to enter the sea and complete a journey that likely started a couple of weeks earlier high in the Eyre Mountains. The river used its last gasp of gravity to push against the rolling surf, momentarily causing the waves to rear up, leaving a veil of spray, before crashing onto the bar.

A trig station, looking like a woman with a metal skirt and a rusted Ned Kelly headpiece, stood defiantly above the tussock staring into the abyss of the Southern Ocean. A long hedge, almost black and moulded smooth by the wind and salt, lay over in submission, growing sideways along the land rather than up towards the sun.

The end of the sandspit lay tantalisingly close, but with no way across the outflow it was time to drive to my starting point six kilometres west on Toetoes Bay. We left the bitumen road for a gravel track before reaching a padlocked gate at the start of the rough track along the sandspit. I changed into walking clothes and put on boots to the sound of the wind and the boom of waves crashing onto the beach on the far side of the dunes. Izzy and Knut, our two West Highland terriers, looked at me in that way dogs often do when they sense change is in the air before they lost interest and headed off to investigate the odours coming off this salty land. I hugged Sue but found it hard to look her in the face. I ruffled my hand over the dogs who sniffed at my boots, stood at the gate while Sue took some photographs, and headed down the track at the start of the walk. I walked backwards for a while waving and watching the Jeep head away, wiped away a tear that had slid below my sunglasses, tightened the belly strap on my pack and lengthened my stride. I was underway.

I walked beside the last meanders of the river towards the estuary where the fresh water waited on its turn to meet the ocean. Wetlands extended north from the far bank, while my path was through rank grasses and rushes. The land here is almost flat, and without the push of gravity, the snake-like curves almost come back on themselves, as though the river is procrastinating, unwilling perhaps to be lost to the ocean.

Whitebaiters' huts lined both sides of the river — a cobbled-together village, made mostly of rusted corrugated iron, windows, doors and some timber as though a scrap yard had been taken from Invercargill and reassembled here on the banks of the Mataura. Some of the huts had grown almost organically from old caravans, glued together by mould and rust. A couple of weary-looking passenger buses added to the collection, sprouting wind-bent television aerials and chimneys, while long grass looked as though it would inexorably pull the whole lot back into the peaty soil.

Faded lounge chairs sat behind glassed-in decks, seats bulging as though the springs were about to break free of the threadbare material. The huts reminded me of the day-dwellings on garden allotments on the outskirts of London I saw from a train window as I commuted to work in the 1970s. These hundred or more temporary dwellings invariably faced the river, looking towards tenuous wooden decks that protruded over the broad, faintly tea-coloured flow. Pulleys and net frames were tied up ready for the next whitebait season when the juvenile fish would enter the river in search of the diminishing wetland habitat they need to survive. Most of the huts had names nailed above their entrances — family names, names reflecting the fishy dreams of their owners, and ironic names reflecting the tough weather that pummels this coast. Most of the huts were surrounded by long grass, some leaned into sheltering flax bushes, and a few had well-tended lawns and beds of summer flowers.

I peered through a couple of windows. Faded, curled girlie calendars hung on some walls, but the huts were mostly well cared for, with the modest utilitarian look of an earlier New Zealand. Like Māori centuries before them, the people who occupy these huts come seasonally to collect food from the river. While I find it hard to imagine how such an odd collection of buildings would be allowed in this age of resource consents, the village looks as though it was meant to be there. I suspect that this community, made up mostly of Southlanders, many retired with time to spare, and others such as farmers, retailers and workers of every sort, know and care more about the health of the river and the catchment that supports the whitebait than most. The huts tend to be handed down from one generation to another; so too, I imagine, is the love of the river and the whitebait that draws people here.

After walking for half an hour along quad-bike tracks in the sand I left the huts behind. I followed the sound of the surf as I climbed through the dunes and stepped onto the steep beach that ran east and west along Toetoes Bay for almost as far as I could see. In the windblown haze I could make out the low profile of Ruapuke Island, former stronghold of the Māori chief Tūhawaiki, and beyond that, the dark mass of Stewart Island. Sun began to push holes through the passing clouds, turning the ocean a deceptively tropical blue. This was not, however, a beach I was drawn to swim from. Heavy surf reared up just twenty metres from the shore before releasing its energy in a shuddering dump, heaving golden fragments of shells up the beach before pulling them back with a hiss that was momentarily louder than the wind that kept the whole process in motion.

Mine were the only footprints on the sand. Further up the beach was the windblown outline of bike tracks, while ahead lay a weathered tyre, but as I walked east on the hard damp edge of the sand, close to the extremity of the fingers of surf, there were no other signs of human activity. I smeared on sunscreen, licked my salty lips, and tied the chin strap on my hat to stop it from flying to South America.

Many of the beaches I have walked on in tropical locations are near densely populated towns and cities, and as a consequence are partly spoiled by the plastic detritus that gathers around the high-tide mark like the soapy smudge line on a dirty bath. The ocean that shapes the beach at Toetoes Bay slides towards us eastward below Africa, along the southern edge of the Indian Ocean, through the roaring band of wind below Australia, and is largely unsullied by humans. As a consequence, this beach was as clean as any I have walked on.

I walked along the beach for half an hour before the emptiness of the land and the sea stretching into the infinity of the Southern Ocean felt oppressive. Charles Brasch wrote of the 'epic southern prairies' as he looked at the same ocean from his home in Dunedin, and I felt I knew what he meant. I grew up surrounded by the rolling hills and mountains of Southland. They provided a comforting edge to my existence, while the openness of the ocean leaves me on the fine edge between wonder and desolation. I remember a friend telling me about his first trip to the sea. We were in our early years at primary school, and my friend lived on a small farm. The sea was so foreign to him that he excitedly described it as looking like hundreds of paddocks covered with water. At the time I had no idea how shaped we were by the early landscapes of our lives.

As the wind tore at my face, I started a mumbling conversation with myself, a buffer perhaps against the loneliness I felt, but it wasn't enough and before long I left the beach for the sand dunes. The high dunes on Toetoes Bay are held together by sand-binding grasses as they roll away from the ocean, mimicking the shape of the waves that have worked with the wind to sculpt them. They sheltered me from the wind and created spaces for ground-hugging plants that angled tiny yellow and blue flowers towards the sun. The whitebaiters' huts, visible again beside the estuary, added a human touch to the place and eased the sense I had on the ocean side that I was walking on the edge of an abyss.

The weight and balance of my new pack felt good and the walking was comfortable away from the wind. About a third of the way down the spit I left the whitebaiters' huts behind and followed a sandy track that looked rarely used. An hour and a half later I reached the narrow eastern end of the sandy peninsula. I looked at my watch and calculated that I had covered about four kilometres an hour — about the pace I needed to maintain to reach my target of twenty kilometres a day. I was heartened by the ease of it.

The township of Fortrose nestled into the rising ground across the estuary. I could see a few campervans parked on the far edge of the estuary and children playing in the water, the sound of their laughter carrying towards me. I leaned my pack into the wiry grass, took off my boots, and clambered down the steep edge of the dunes onto the wet granular bed of the estuary. The ebb of the tide quickened, pulling the river past me, the low hiss of its flow just audible against the roar of the ocean hidden beyond the dunes. The current unfurled vortices of sand from the bottom, leaving on the exposed bed a series of perfect wave-like shapes, broken only by the prints of my bare feet. I held my camera close to the sand in an attempt to capture the beauty of it before walking to the place where the Mataura left the land and joined the ocean. The wild clash of river and surf at the bar unleashed plumes of spray into the hazy sky.

I sat on a piece of driftwood and watched the river and the ocean merge, thinking for a moment about how long it took for the rain in the Eyre Mountains to find its way here, and whether any of this departing water would ever make the same journey — evaporated from the ocean by the sun, somewhere west of New Zealand, before being piled up as cloud against the mountains, to start the process all over again. The odds looked slim, even allowing the process a billion years to happen.

A couple of stocky black oystercatchers noisily clacked red beaks at me and strutted around my seat on the log, sending a signal that this was their place. A fish left a hefty swirl on the edge of the flow. Black-backed gulls surfed the currents of wind along the frayed edge of the surf and dunes, once in a while dropping urgently to grab something exposed in the flux.

I set up my tent in the sand nestled between the dunes. The lightweight Big Agnes tent was new. While I had erected it several times at home where the only obstacle was a tumbling grandchild or a nosy terrier, I hadn't put it up in the wind. For a moment it looked as though my fly might follow the river to the ocean. After quelling the unruly fly, I turned away from the rest of the tent long enough for it to lift like a hovercraft and attempt an escape. What had taken three or four minutes in the backyard took close to ten to establish in the dunes.

While I was setting up my gas stove and choosing a pack of dried venison risotto for dinner, I thought it would be both tasty and fitting to add some food from the estuary to the pot. A line of pied oystercatchers dipped their long beaks into the sand at the edge of the departing water while I scooped a handful of clams from the sand and washed them in the salty water. In the brief time it took for the water to boil, and the dried risotto to swell into something that looked edible, the clams opened, leaking their salty flavour into the dish. I ate the food from the billy while sitting on the high point of a dune, observing the colours desert the estuary and wetlands in the north. I was about to discard the clam shells when I decided to carry a pair of them up the river and deposit them in the headwaters — as my koha to the river.

I walked back to the river mouth to watch the sun drop through layers of cloud before the turn of the earth made it look as though it had descended into the cold ocean. Across the estuary a couple walked beside the full outward rush of the tide.

He cast a lure in the water but hooked nothing. Behind them the black skeletal ribs of an old shipwreck came out of the sand, like the long fingers of a hand, clawing towards the sky. This is a coast that has seen a number of shipping disasters: in 1881 the S.S. *Tararua* was wrecked at Waipapa Point, ten kilometres east of Fortrose, and ten of the 131 who perished are buried in the town's cemetery.

One day, back in the 1830s, eleven southern right whales were killed near here before being dragged over the sand bar close to where I stood and rendered down for oil at Fortrose. It was reported that much of the oil became rancid before it could be transported from the district, leaving most of the haul wasted. Within a couple of decades, the migration of right whales along this coast had been all but extinguished.

Sandflies emerged as the wind dropped. Because I hadn't expected to encounter them until I reached the mountains to the north I had left the repellent behind. I slapped a few and outpaced the rest with a brisk walk. Red- and black-billed gulls searched for food across the slowing outward flow, while two royal spoonbills scythed their long, rounded bills through the shallows, the tufts of white feathers on their heads waving in the breeze, like a bad comb-over. Dozens of oystercatchers probed the watery edge of the flats; summer voices floated across the estuary from a bonfire built on the beach.

Around dark, which arrived after ten, I crawled into my sleeping bag, closed the tent zip, squashed the sandflies that joined me, wrote some notes about the day's walk, and fell asleep while reading *As I Walked Out One Midsummer Morning*. Lee's journey started optimistically, on a dusty road, heading for Spain by way of London, hazel stick in his hand and violin under an arm.

Just after five, in the grey half-light of morning, I woke to the sound of a rooster crowing from across the water. I had a sleepy recollection of the sound of rain on the tent in the night, but as

I lay in my warm bag I sensed the wind had gone. The sides of the tent were still, and the sound of the ocean had changed — its constant roar was replaced by a silence, broken about every ten seconds by the boom of surf, as though a distant battle was being fought with a battery of cannons.

I stretched my stiff body in the cool air as this far corner of the planet turned once more towards the sun, colouring the cloud in the south-east shades of apricot and grey. By seven I had packed my tent, eaten breakfast of muesli and brewed coffee. I walked back to the river and sloshed the brackish water over my face before plucking up the courage to remove my clothes and ease my naked body chest-deep into the flow, hoping that no one in the campervans was scanning the estuary with binoculars.

By seven-thirty I had started my walk proper, heading away from the river mouth and towards the high country to the north. If I was able to maintain the pace I hoped for, I would reach the source of the river in twelve days. In the optimistic dawn, my mind raced forward to a sunny mountain slope beside the gurgling birth of the Mataura, as though it could be reached without hardship and disappointment. Initially I retraced the remnant track through the dunes where a myriad of desert-like plants and leathery rock-hugging lichens flourished between the dune grasses. The bleached shells of large snails littered the ground in places.

About halfway along the sandspit I crossed the dunes and walked onto the beach. With the storm-driven haze of the previous day gone, Ruapuke Island, twenty kilometres south, was clearly visible. Two hundred Māori lived on the island when it was the stronghold of the Ngāi Tahu chief Tūhawaiki. The low-lying Titi or Mutton Bird islands were also visible slightly south-west of Ruapuke; further west, Stewart Island and Bluff Hill stood out from the ocean. The tall chimney of the aluminium smelter at Tiwai Point was the only sign of human activity.

The sandy beach I walked on, and the dunes behind me, felt fragile in the face of the Southern Ocean. Before my walk I had read Nicolas Crane's *The Making of the British Landscape: from the Ice Age to the present*. It jolted my sense of what was fixed or timeless in a landscape — my default setting that what I see is solid and unchanging, even though intellectually I know we live on a planet of constant change. I could understand a combination of storms and rising sea levels tearing the sandspit apart, but what I found more difficult to accept was that if I had been walking here just 10,000 years earlier the land would have stretched south, beyond the current horizon. Back then the islands to the south would have been part of the land-mass of the South Island. For a moment I contemplated where the coastline would be in another 5000 years. If current predictions for this warming planet are correct, the sandspit, whitebaiters' huts and the wetlands beyond would be gone within a hundred years.

Because I guessed I would need the rest, I decided to take a break every hour to eat and spend time contemplating the walk. As the first hour came to an end, I saw two dolphins swimming towards me, about fifty metres out in Foveaux Strait. Their presence diminished the emptiness I felt. I took off my pack, sat on the sun-warmed sand and grabbed the first of the zip-lock bags of nuts I had filled for my trip. The dolphins swam away to the east for about a hundred metres before turning towards the beach, and headed back in my direction. Out of curiosity I walked to the edge of the surf and watched them as they angled towards me, as though they had seen me, or sensed the vibration of my footfall. They passed just twenty metres out, elegantly breaking through the slick surface, exposing their rounded dorsal fins and velvet flanks, dark on top with creamy undersides, so close together they looked like lovers. Eventually the rare little Hector's dolphins turned away from the beach, leaving me feeling better for the encounter.

LEAVING THE SANDSPIT

I followed the beach for half an hour before recrossing the dunes towards the whitebaiters' huts. My meagre water supplies were exhausted, and while my clever little water filter was able to remove bacteria and most viruses from fresh water, I hadn't counted on the need to remove salt from the brackish water of the lower Mataura. Most huts had rooftop rain-collection systems, and I hoped to access one of the tanks, but the first few I looked at appeared to have taps that could only be opened from inside the buildings. Eventually I found a tank with a screw cap on top which I removed, and dipped my container into the water. I drank it in great gulps, not thinking until I was finished that it might have been wise to suck it through the filter.

Before leaving the sandspit I climbed back onto the dunes to get a better look at the land to the north. Beyond the estuary lay an expanse of low rolling country that looked as though it had only just made it out of the sea. A few kilometres west towards Waituna Lagoon lay a myriad of waterways surrounded by swamp grasses, flaxes and patches of native bush. This almost impenetrable land would have stretched beyond the horizon in the north before the arrival of Europeans in the middle of the nineteenth century. The Waituna Lagoon is now hemmed in by intensive farming and the water flowing into this vast wetland is enriched with fertiliser. Beyond Tokanui, on the eastern side of the river, dark bush-covered highlands give way to rough hills, sliced by a myriad of creeks and streams, grassed on the smooth faces, while remnant native bush fills the gullies. On the horizon to the north lie the Hokonui Hills. Until I was seventeen and left Gore for university in Dunedin, they formed the backdrop of my life. All going well, I hoped to reach them in four days.

Māori were the first to travel from the coast to their seasonal settlements at Tuturau and the Mataura Falls. Whalers reached this southern coast in the 1830s but it took a further twenty years for the first European explorers to reach the Mataura near Gore. Many were reported to have looked at the prospect of heading inland but were deterred by the harsh climate and the swathe of boggy land that formed a barrier between the coast and the Hokonui Hills. Some, however, thought the land looked promising. In *Pioneer Recollections*, James Herries Beattie reports on a visit in 1843 by Mr F. Tuckett, a surveyor appointed by the Free Church Association of Scotland to find a place for settlement in the 'middle island' of New Zealand. He said that, as he looked north at the land he was about to cross, 'as far as I could see north-east, certainly beyond Tuturau, the land appeared to be one continued prairie, not low and flat nor much broken, but a fine swelling surface, slightly elevated, just a surface as is most compatible with beauty and utility'. Tuckett didn't last, however. He encountered a cold wet winter and decided to settle further north.

For the first couple of hours I walked into a warm breeze from the north, listening to the rhythmic creaking of my pack and the crunch of boots on sand and gravel. Near a boat-launching ramp I saw a vehicle and trailer which served to amplify the strange emptiness of the place. A few lawns around the huts had been recently cut, but the huts themselves were deserted, as though a plague had swept the land.

Beyond the estuary the peat-stained river ran beside a path of white gravel. The stable banks of this tidal section of the river are made of soft brown mud, with weed beds fringing the watery edge. The river loops through the flat land, the current passing quietly, like a thief in the night, between banks tangled with willows and chest-high grasses.

After a couple of hours I climbed onto a whitebait stand and sat, perched over the water, making coffee and eating an energy bar. A mob of mallards watched me from a distance, and once in a while pūkeko would appear along the reedy edge of the river. Tiny fish splashed around the shallows; blue and red damsel flies skimmed the slick surface. Tired, I lay on the wooden slats of the stand, stretched my legs, and looked at the high cirrus above, patterned to resemble the rippled shapes left on the sand by the falling tide. A mallard made a low pass over the stand, and tiny black swallows darted about, almost close enough to touch. My eyes closed, and for a moment I drifted into a light sleep.

My upstream path followed the gravel on Holz Road, the river tight in on my right, and a sheep farm to the west between my route and the Waituna Wetlands. I waved at a farmer on a tractor topping thistles. He stopped and walked over to the fence, as though he was looking for company in this otherwise empty place. He looked fit, around forty, and wore an All Blacks jersey.

'Beautiful day,' I said.

'Sure is. We deserve some after the shit of the last few weeks. What are you up to?' he asked with a smile.

'I'm on the first day of a walk up the Mataura. All the way to the Eyre Mountains. At least, that's the plan.'

'Bingo to that,' he said. 'Forecast looks a bit dodgy though, mate.'

Caged dogs barked as I passed a farmhouse, and washing

flapped on long sagging lines in the warm wind. The house had a tough, frontier look about it, as though civilisation had a loose grip near this wild coast. At lunchtime I stepped off the road, swung my pack to the ground and lay in the high grass between the river and the road. I checked the topographical map for progress, and thought about possible routes upstream in the afternoon. The sound of a truck rumbling down the road woke me from a shallow sleep, and as I pushed the hat from my face I saw for a split-second the driver high above me in the cab of his stock truck before I was enveloped in a cloud of dust that carried with it the smell of sheep shit. The high, benevolent cirrus of the morning had been transformed into a layer of steel-grey cloud, and as I readied to move on I felt the first spots of rain on my dusty face.

A kilometre up the road I reached the first bridge over the Mataura — a utilitarian concrete structure on the Tokanui Gorge Road.

The map showed the river parting company with all roads for the next twenty kilometres. My plan was to leave the road and follow the western bank of the river as far as a disused railway bridge about six kilometres upstream, where I intended to pitch my tent. I was heading into dairy-farming country for the first time on the walk, and had an uneasiness about confronting the electric fences that I imagined lay in wait.

Getting off the bridge proved a challenge. An electric wire ran right to its abutment, and the tiny gap between the insulator and the bridge, if I had been able to squeeze through, would have dropped me into an impenetrable tangle of vegetation. Upstream I could see a farm track running along the top of a flood-bank, but the only practical way to reach it required a brief excursion over private land. With no farmhouse nearby where I could seek permission to cross the land, I felt I had no alternative but to slither under the bottom wire of the electric fence and take my chances across the farmland. I feel like I'm a school boy again stealing apples when I walk over land without first receiving permission. It's mostly irrational, because in all the time I have walked beside rivers I have been ordered off the property only half a dozen times — but the fear and vulnerability I feel remains.

For an hour I continued upstream along top of the flood-bank, making good progress on the heavily grazed ground. The Mataura flowed close by through a series of gentle curves, its banks less impacted by the tides than they were downstream. The flow, though, remained dark and the river rolled past without sound. Hundreds of mallard ducks floated on a slow pool, cackling as though there was much gossip to impart that summer afternoon.

Every few hundred metres I had to take off my pack and slide under another electric fence. After more than six hours on the move my legs had lost their bounce, and the milestones on my map which earlier in the day I reached with ease now took longer than expected. For much of this section of the walk the electric fence that ran parallel to the river butted hard up against the willows, leaving no way of navigating upstream without getting onto the paddocks. Gorse, broom and chest-high grasses filled those areas of the riparian margin not strangled with willows. Walking along this right of passage would have required a machete. The fences, though, keep cows from the riverbanks, and the jungle of foliage that has grown up between them and the river will act to trap some of the nutrient-rich run-off from the land — but access to the river is increasingly being lost.

Three or four kilometres from my planned camping spot I walked a section of the riverbank where the electric fences were further back from the water. Because sheep had been able to get under the fence the roughest of the growth had been kept in check, allowing me to walk beside the river. Discouragingly, there were cows in this section, and while they were mostly kept away from the river by a single strand of electric tape, in places the tape had been flattened by fallen branches, allowing the cows to break down sections of riverbank.

Looking south from the top of the flood-bank I could see the swampy edge of the Waituna Wetlands and the last substantial stands of remnant forest in the area, while I was surrounded by a sea of emerald-green grassland stretching upstream towards the horizon. A few beech trees stood in clusters of twos and threes, frayed by wind with the protective shield of the forest removed. I wondered why they had been spared when the land was cleared. Perhaps the landowners a century or so ago decided that it would be good to leave a reminder of what went before, but when I looked at them, in the middle of dairy paddocks, I was saddened by these lonely-looking sentinels that served to heighten my sense of what had been lost.

I was twenty kilometres into my walk before I saw the first person on the river. The angler pushed his way out of a tangle of broom and willows and walked towards me before stopping, then retreated again into the vegetation. By then I was keen to talk with someone other than myself and was puzzled by his behaviour, which suggested he wasn't looking for company. A few minutes later he reappeared, studied the ground in front of him closely before clambering under an electric fence and heading my way. 'Sorry, I realised I had lost my sunglasses. Needed to look for them,' he said.

'Had me worried for a moment. Thought I might have scared you off.'

'No, my glasses must have been ripped off the cord while I was scrambling through all that broom. Wouldn't normally worry, but they cost hundreds of bucks. Prescription,' he said.

'And did you find them?'

'No. I'll go back and look again.'

'How was the fishing?' I asked.

'Found some good fish, and caught a few. Haven't been here before and wasn't sure what to expect. I usually fish further upstream, but saw on a map that there was an old public road down here. Thought I would give it a try.'

'You live around here?' I asked.

'Just outside Invercargill. Used to live in Dunedin. I was an engineer at Scotts. Moved to Christchurch with them a long time back. Then the earthquake came along, my girls grew up and didn't need me close by — and my wife left me. Time for a change. Worked in Western Australia for a while, but I was drawn back. I'm originally from Ireland. Wanted to get as far south as I could, near the rivers. Came back to find I had prostate cancer. Tough treatment, but they say I'm good now. Spend most of my time fishing.'

He was about my age, and some elements of his life trajectory weren't that different from mine. 'Did you know Bill McLay back in Dunedin?' I asked. Bill was my fishing mentor and friend, as well as an engineer in Dunedin forty years back.

'Only met Bill once,' he said. 'Heard he was an extraordinary fisherman. I fished the Gold Medal a few times. Mike Weddell kept winning it back then.'

'I've fished with Mike over the years. Close to perfection with a fly rod,' I said.

He headed back to the undergrowth while I walked on past a disused rail bridge hanging over the river like a rusting sculpture, each end severed from the land. The bridge was constructed in the early 1890s as part of the Tokanui branch line that ran south-east from Invercargill. Its early freight was timber taken from the newly settled land, and fertiliser back to the cleared land — as well as passengers and produce in both directions. The port at Fortrose lost trade to the railway and closed, while the railway line survived until 1966. The old bridge must be one of the earliest man-made structures still visible near the river, its slow decay witnessed by just the odd angler, a farmer or two, and hundreds of dairy cows.

Towering cumulus strode across the sky as I climbed off the

flood-bank in the early evening and pushed through grass and thistles that reached my shoulders while I searched for a camping spot by the river. On a sliver of grassy bank in the lee of a cluster of willows I pitched my tent just a metre from the water. The jaunty optimism I felt for the first hours of the day had left me like a slow leak, my legs were dead tired, and the adventurous spirit I had imagined I would feel had been replaced by doubt about the sense of my walk. The wind building from the west carried the smell of cow shit instead of the sweet smell of newly mown hay and the honeyed air from clover rich pasture — the things I had romantically associated with camping near the river in summer. And the river too felt alien, with its heavy dark flow running between high willow-cloaked banks. It felt like a small version of the Mississippi that I knew from reading *The Adventures of Huckleberry Finn* — brooding, and mysterious, and not much like the river I knew and loved further north.

Stripped down to my underpants I clambered over the bank, grimaced briefly, and hoped my heart wouldn't burst as I lowered myself into the current to wash away the day's sweat. Once my body accepted the cold I lay with my nose close to the slick flow and watched a couple of adult caddis flies walk over the surface, as though it was made of metal. A small trout started rising a couple of metres above me, and off to my right, as though startled by my white legs dangling in the current, a large trout surged out of a deep run and tried to shimmy its way over a gravel bar so shallow the bulk of its back was out of the water. It was a strange reversal of things — me in the water, hanging on awkwardly, and the trout looking disorientated by being mostly out of the water. It took some vigorous tail-thrashing before it made it to deeper water and headed upstream, pushing a bow-wave ahead as though it was a small submarine. It looked so out of place I assumed it had recently arrived from the ocean and, like me, was finding its way upstream.

I dried off using a travel towel that wanted to stick to my body, or push droplets of water about as though it hadn't learned that its task was to absorb the water. In the end I stood naked on the bank and dried in the wind while watching ominous clouds building in the evening sky. I boiled a two-serve pack of dried honey chicken with soy but it fell short, both in taste and texture, of the fraudulent mouth-watering expectations created by the image on the pack.

The nature of the river by my camp had changed from the mud-banked estuarine channel just a few kilometres downstream. The long slow pools of the lower river remained, but gravel and rock bars at the tail of the pools created a different architecture on the surface — ripples and small waves appeared, and the accelerated flow over these obstructions gave the river its voice. That unmistakable but difficult to define gurgle and hiss.

On dusk I watched the dimpling rises of a few trout as they took insects from the flat pool beside the tent, but the long walk, and the effort involved in setting up my modest camp, left me too drained to fish. Eventually I slid into my sleeping bag, lay back on a pillow made of my few clothes stuffed inside my jersey and was transported to Spain in the 1930s and Laurie Lee's walking tour, sleeping in the open on the high plains or in warm village beds with the young, and not so young, women he claimed to have met on the way. This romantic version of a walk across Spain by a nineteen-year-old felt a world away from mine, approaching sixty-eight and walking through dairy farms. By the time I put my book down thunderous rain and wind flailed my tent.

The shooting started as I was about to fall asleep. Loud cracks that reverberated through the storm, at times close, sounded as though they were coming from the top of the flood-bank. My heart thudded — I couldn't imagine anyone shooting hares or rabbits in that tempest. This had happened to me before, in a tent alone near the roadside south of Jackson, on the way to the

Cascade. Back then I was woken by shots and a powerful beam of light that threw shadows over my tent. The next morning I found the unwanted remains of a deer in a bloody heap by the road, only fifty metres from my tent.

This night the shooting eventually died away in the storm and, after worrying briefly about being so close to the river in the rain, I drifted into a dream-tossed sleep.

HEADED FOR WYNDHAM

My back, which wasn't used to being separated from the ground by something as flimsy as a self-inflating mattress, woke me early. As the sun climbed in the east, warming my tent with a light turned pale orange by my colourful tent fly, I opened the map and planned the day. I laid a piece of twine, cut to represent twenty kilometres on the map, along the curves of the river to find my likely destination. Covering twenty kilometres had appeared an easy target from the comfort of home, but my early experience with the weight of the pack, electric fences, and the leg-sapping vegetation encountered along the riparian strip made it feel a slog. I decided to track along the western bank of the river for about ten kilometres before following McCall Road as far as the Mataura Island bridge. Depending on progress I planned then to make a call as to how closely to follow the river beyond the bridge, before ending the day about four kilometres south of Wyndham.

Two black-backed gulls flew upstream, eyes scanning the surface of the river, while I ate cereal and drank a strong brew of coffee, my legs dangling over the riverbank, almost touching the flow.

I moved north along the top of an ungrazed flood-bank and was quickly drenched to the waist by the thistles, docks and long grasses that drooped under the weight of the previous night's rain. The rolling hills of Forest Range pushed fingers of native bush towards the river in the east, but with few exceptions the land on the broad river flats was a monoculture of grass and winter feed for dairy cows. There was a green lush beauty in it though, seen through the diamond clarity of air swept clean by an ocean seemingly without end.

A steep scrub-covered bank forced me to climb away from the river. From the top of the chest-heaving rise I could see what appeared to be several kilometres of easy walking. The Hokonui Hills remained my initial target, a couple of days' walk to the north. The mild breeze of morning had given way to a westerly gale and behind me, towards the coast, another squall line of clouds galloped over the land. Rising ground, a patch of rough bush, and a three-strand electric fence pushed me further from the river, before a dip in the ground allowed me to slip precariously under the lower wire and make my way down a steep muddy slide to the water. After an hour's walk I lay in the grass against a shelter belt of trees and ate a chocolate-almond fudge bar. Large raindrops thudded into my jacket as I phoned Sue to catch up on news from home. She told me the dogs were bored and missed me, but I knew it wasn't true. I'm too often away on fishing trips, and I suspect they have seen right through my lack of reliability. We made plans to meet in Mataura to top up my supplies at the end of the following day.

For an hour and a half my track was close to the river, mostly along the overgrown riparian margin, but at times I was forced back onto the paddocks where once again I had to remove my pack every ten minutes or so and slide under the wires. Despite the strength-sapping effort required to navigate the fences, I was impressed that the river was fenced off along this entire section, as were the creeks and swales that joined it. As a consequence, there was no sign of stock damage to the banks.

The soft curious eyes of Friesian cows followed me, but apart from a farm worker on a distant quad bike I didn't see another person. A few prosperous-looking houses angled towards the river from a terrace a couple of kilometres west, but most faced towards the sun and away from the river.

My progress was halted by a spring creek that flowed in from the west. It was surrounded by a fine example of the effort that has been put in to fence the streams and, in this case at least, the planting of native species to restore habitat. After sliding under the fence, I pushed through a protective planting of flax and tussock before reaching the creek. My attempt to cross it near the Mataura was thwarted by the jelly-like mud that alarmingly reached my thighs as soon as I ventured into it. I bench-pressed my pack back up the high bank and used the long grass to slowly extract my legs from the sucking mud. With my trousers carrying an outer layer of mud and stinking cow shit from the regular belly slides under the fences, I trudged up the bank of the creek looking for a more satisfactory crossing. After fifteen minutes I found an unused wooden bridge, grass sprouting between its rotten planks. I crossed it, one tentative step after another, dragging my pack behind to reduce the weight of my steps on the suspect planks.

As I walked away from the coast the look of the river changed with the subtle alteration to its rate of descent. Gravel beaches appeared with increasing frequency along with ripples, runs and pools. It started looking more like parts of the river I was familiar with upstream. I had fished here before, perhaps thirty years earlier. A healthy population of mature mayfly nymphs, cased caddis and tiny snails grazed on the thin layer of algae that covered the stones I turned over in a couple of ripples. The stream bottom looked cleaner with less smothering filamentous algae than I recalled from decades earlier. I drank from the river, using my filter bottle. The water in this part of river has a distinctive musty taste that can also be found in the flesh of trout. The taste and smell of it brought back a flood of memories — mostly of evenings spent swimming in the river near Gore, when taking in the odd gulp was inevitable. The river in this area is large — too big to safely wade across, and the heavily willowed banks and lack of open gravel beaches would make upstream fly-fishing for trout difficult.

By the time I reached the track leading on to McCall Road, anvil-headed storm clouds rolled across the sky with curtains of rain and hail draped along the squall lines. I huddled in the wet grass to escape the worst of the wind, drank steaming coffee, and ate salami and nuts for lunch. Between squalls I studied the map and thought about my route towards Wyndham. My plan had been to follow the river as it curved eastward, away from the Island Edendale Road, towards the partially bush-clad country north of Kuriwao Hill, setting up camp by the river a few kilometres south of Wyndham. However, the howling wind, rough vegetation close to the river, and my increasingly sore heels had started to wear me down, making the thought of camping in the rain unappealing. In hope of reaching Wyndham by the end of the day, I decided to leave the riverbank and follow the road, believing that the easier walking would allow me to cover the extra distance to Wyndham. I felt a pang of guilt at being away from the river, but figured that because the stretch was so heavily willowed it would have been impossible for me to have stayed on the bank. Another ten kilometres of walking interrupted every few hundred metres by electric fences had no appeal — the three jolts that had already whacked my hand and pounced on my damp backside had rattled me.

My heels ached when I started walking after each hourly rest, leaving me to hobble along until numbness set in. The combination of fishing boots and neoprene inners had allowed my feet to slip about, and I became anxious about developing blisters. In the shelter of a hedgerow I called the Wyndham

Hotel and made a booking for the night, the thought of a warm shower and soft bed irresistible.

I leaned into the gale that, at times, caught my pack and threatened to throw me from the road, eventually reaching Menzies Ferry with throbbing heels and leaden legs. The sky had cleared when I sprawled under a large tree in the grounds of the war memorial. I pulled off my boots and inners, squeezed the water from my socks and looked up at the statue of a soldier from the Great War, backlit by the sun, his young face looking past me towards the river in the east. I ate an energy bar while five pīwakawaka cavorted in a tree. I rubbed my cracked heels, relieved that no blisters had formed, before hobbling over to the deserted tennis court next to the memorial. Grass grew up through the asphalt, as did moss on the nets which looked as though they had drooped across the courts for a decade or two. Back at the monument I read the names of the thirteen young men from this small farming district who were killed in World War I, and thought about the serendipitous timing of my lucky life. There was beauty in the statue and shelter from the wind, and something else less easily defined about the place that caused me to linger. As I left Menzies Ferry — now just a road sign, intersection, a couple of houses and hall — I noticed on a plaque that the hall was completed in 1913, and thought about the patriotic celebrations that probably took place there when the soldiers left the district to fight for the Empire. The images stayed with me for a time as I headed towards the river down Ferry Factory Road, along with the disconcerting image of grief that would have followed, in the case of the thirteen who didn't come back, and the fractured existence of the survivors as they tried to make sense of what they had seen — and done.

The gigantic drying towers at Fonterra's milk-processing plant at Edendale climbed into the sky ahead, in clear disparity to the rolling landscape, and the few farmhouses and milking sheds that dotted the land. The plant, one of the largest in the world, stands over the land as a cathedral might have dominated the landscape in medieval England, but in this case it's a monument to another religion — industrial-scale processing and global trade. At the peak of the season, coal-fired heat from its boilers drives the moisture from sixteen million litres of milk a day. Some of it left in the plume of steam visible above the plant as I trekked north.

Three kilometres downstream of the Wyndham bridge the nature of the river changed. Gravel beaches and ripples appeared every few hundred metres, and the willow-choked banks gave way to low grasses. Walking became easy, and I began to feel as though I was walking beside an old friend.

Late in the afternoon I left the river beside Wyndham and gratefully threw my pack on the back of a ute when offered a ride over the bridge into town. The man who picked me up was the first person I had seen to talk to that day.

'How far have you walked?' he asked.

'Started three days ago, near Fortrose. My plan is to walk up the river.'

'Good on ya. Some slog, though. Where do you want dropped?'

'Hotel would be great, thanks,' I answered.

'Might see you there later. Been married forty-three years today. Gonna let the missus decide where we'll celebrate.'

I deposited my pack in the room, removed my boots and, because I wasn't carrying spare shoes, decided to go straight to the bar in clean socks. I often feel awkward walking into a country bar, and this one wasn't an exception. A drinker sat at each end of the L-shaped bar, while another three men sat around a high table with jugs, riveted to horse races beamed in from some far-off place. The patrons glanced at me in my dirty trousers and shoeless feet then went back to the races and their beer.

I perched on a stool between the two at the bar.

'Gidday. You look buggered,' said Lean, the guy on my left. He was lean with irregular teeth in gums that looked as though they had shrunken as he aged. He gave the impression of having lived a big life, not all of it easy.

'Walking up the river, started at the coast. I'm headed all the way to the source, up in the Eyre Mountains,' I said, hoping to explain my arrival.

'Hell of a walk. Took my granddaughters fishing near Garston once. River's crystal-clear up there,' he said, as though he was talking about another country. 'The girls kick my arse now when we go fishing. What do you think of the river?'

'Better than I recall it was when I came here years ago. Cleaner bottom now, and mostly well fenced to keep the cows out.'

'Great to hear,' he said, smiling. 'All we fucken hear are stories about how dairying is buggering the rivers.'

After a while he looked past me. 'I've got some pigs to kill tomorrow.'

His mate looked at him and said, 'Yeah?'

'I use the pens down that road by the river.'

His mate looked at me with a smirk. 'I know the place. Used to call it lovers' lane. Went down there Friday nights when I was a kid. Bare legs and trousers hanging out of cars all over the place,' he said with a grin. 'They chased us off.' He laughed, then looked down at his beer.

'Had trouble killing the last one,' said Lean. 'Wouldn't come down the chute far enough to let me have a clean shot at it. What a fucken racket. Finally held a sheep nut in front of it. Fucker moved forward enough so I could get a shot at it.'

'Yeah,' said his mate.

'Got six to kill in the morning. Well, I'm helping Joe. I'm not that bloody good at it. You want to help?'

'What time?'

'About eight.'

'Bit bloody early.' Then silence, followed by: 'Okay, see you there.'

Lean said he had to go. He paid the barmaid, wished me good luck, and left with a carton of Green Antler under his arm.

I asked the barmaid if they had many fishermen staying at the hotel these days.

'An American guy stays here some years. Can't think of anyone else.'

'This part of the river was once a Mecca for foreign anglers. Back in the 1960s I think many of them used Wyndham as a base,' I said.

'There were a lot of old photos of fishermen on the wall in the dining room, but they were taken down when we refurbished the place. Not sure where they ended up.'

'You from here?' I asked.

'My husband is, but I'm from up north. Been here about six years now. Love the place. Couldn't imagine living anywhere else. It's a good community.'

I left the bar to the group watching the races and a boy, who looked as though he might still go to primary school, playing pool.

The hot shower eased my stiff body, tempting me to stay in so long that when I emerged from behind the curtain the bathroom was filled with a soap-smelling fog. I ate alone in the cavernous dining room that smelt of fresh paint and new carpets. Seafood chowder with garlic bread, an oversized steak with chips and salad, followed by a dessert of custard and fruit. The cook, who also served the meals, looked at me as though I might be mad when I told her why I was there.

Outside the rain-streaked window, locals arrived in utes and double-cabs and drove off with cartons of beer. Two young men I had seen earlier, drinking under cover of an outdoor awning so they could smoke, stood on the footpath talking. One of them went into the bottle store while his mate fixed his stare on something down the road and swayed gently, as though he was trying to find his equilibrium. He dropped his bottle in the grass and mouthed some words to his mate who appeared with a carton of Coruba and Coke RTDs before they left, weaving down the footpath.

Over the street the flagpole high on the elegant old Post Office Building — now used as flats — leaned away from the south-west, like most of the trees I passed near the coast. The building had seen better days, like many of the other attractive buildings in the centre of town.

As I left the dining room the cook said, 'Breakfast is included in your charge, but there won't be anyone here when you plan to leave. Come and I'll show you the kitchen. Help yourself to whatever you want — eggs and bacon in the fridge, cereal and bread over there. You don't need me to tell you to sleep well,' she laughed.

'I've come away without a socket for my phone charger. Do you know if there's one in the hotel?' I asked.

'Afraid not, but I have one at home. Happy to go and get it for you.'

'That's way too much, but thank you for the offer. I'm sure I can survive.'

WYNDHAM TO MATAURA

I woke to the sound of rain pounding on the roof. Summers in the south can be brilliant, but sometimes they just don't happen. This was looking like one of those years. By eight-thirty I was leaving the quiet rain-slick streets of Wyndham, happy knowing I would meet Sue later in the day. Before leaving my hotel room I applied plasters to my cracked heels, and decided this would be a day to keep them dry in the hope they would repair.

I walked north on Wyndham Road and, beyond the race-course, crossed the well-fenced peat-stained water of the Mimihau Stream. Bruise-coloured clouds filled the sky behind me, but fifty kilometres to the north the Hokonui Hills climbed into clear blue. Patches of native bush fringed the steeper land to the east; towards the river the land was green and bouncy. While I rejoice when I see these remnant patches of bush, attitudes to the landscape and bush have changed over time. Back in 1894, J. O. McKenzie was quoted in *New Zealand's Treasury of Trout and Salmon* as saying:

This New Zealand has been termed the Britain of the south. There is much to remind of the old home; English trees, shrubs, fruits and flowers in abundance and no scarcity of clouds, rain and wind. Our Otago streams have many features in their surroundings all in common with the Ribble and Tweed; and could we only suppress the ubiquitous flax plant and on yonder cliff, where stands the waving cabbage palm, conjure up the orthodox ruin . . .

This landscape has paid a heavy price for this vision of home on the other side of the planet.

The Mataura curved away in an avenue of willows towards Coal Pit Road, a section of water I first fished thirty years earlier with John Dean, Bill McLay and Mike Weddell. Mayfly hatches set the tone for fishing in this area, regular hatches that attract the attention of astonishing numbers of trout.

The river follows a more consistent course across the land in these lower reaches than it does above Gore. The banks are relatively stable and the bottom made up of larger material than is found where it crosses the broad alluvial Waimea Plains in the north. These larger stones are less easily moved about by floods, and the reefs of exposed rock and lignite add further permanence to the structure of the river. This stability creates a rich habitat for insects and the trout that feed on them. For much of last century this part of the river was recognised as being an outstanding fishery, but its health was fragile because it was subjected to high levels of pollution. The towns that grew along its banks allowed untreated sewage to run to the river, and the meat and dairy processors that operated near it used the Mataura as a drain. When I first knew this part of the river, in the second half of last century, it smelt of human and animal waste, and the stony bottom was often choked with filaments of algae that broke off and drifted in what at times was a soup-like flow. While the river here is far from pristine now, the reduction in point-source pollution that has taken place over the last twenty years has allowed it to survive as a living organism.

It is a testament to the cleansing power of rivers that they can, given a chance, recover from mistreatment.

Towards the end of my first hour I saw a sign pointing down a farm lane to Retro Organics, a local cheesemaker. I was ready for a break, and my mouth watered at the thought of some cheese for lunch. They had a range of organic cheeses for sale, all made from milk sourced from paddocks that surrounded the plant attached to a spartan tasting room. I tried a couple, but my heart was stolen by 'Mataura Tasty', a pale-orange Cheddar named after the river of my life.

The woman who served me saw the fly-rod tube attached to the side of my pack. 'You on a fishing trip?' she asked.

'I'm walking the length of the river. I did think it might have been at least partly a fishing trip, but I realised pretty quickly that it wasn't. Mostly I'm too tired to fish, and I'm enjoying the walk — putting one foot in front of the other, looking at the land.'

She told me she was the secretary of the Mataura Angling Club.

'I've recently read some of the history of the club,' I said. 'How's it going these days?'

'We've ten adult members and four juniors. It's hard to find members, but after years of our numbers going down, we have at least started to hold our own,' she said.

The club sounded as though it was only just surviving, a far cry from its early days. In *Mataura, City of the Falls* I had read of the club's beginnings. It was formed after a meeting of twenty gentlemen considered the advisability of forming an angling club. In 1929, during the Prohibition era, disaster struck: to satisfy the thirst of members at the AGM, the club had procured twenty-seven gallons of ale, which was confiscated by Constable Murphy. Toasts had to be made using Quilters Lemonade. The club secretary and local carrier were fined.

Later, the writer describes a club member being suspicious of the results of one of their competitions. His uncle had caught what he thought to be the winning bag — thirty-three trout. At the last moment in came two fishermen with fifty trout each. The following day the club member, visiting the home of one of the winners, noted that the pair had emptied a five-gallon keg to celebrate their win, and hanging on the fence was a floundering net — still wet.

The 1936 quadrangular tournament between West Otago, Mataura, Wyndham and Gore didn't involve fishing. Instead the clubs met to formulate a plan to combat the contamination of the Mataura River. The cause of the problem was traced to sludge coming from the gold dredges at Waikaka and Waikaia. One member suggested building a dam with a sludge gate to be opened one day a week!

Competition records showed that the number of trout weighed in fell from a high of 375 in 1936 to eight in 1980 and ten in 1990, while the average size of the fish increased from under half a kilo to one and a half kilos. While declining club membership, and the loss of interest in competition fishing, will have been a factor in the reduced numbers of fish weighed in, a decline in water quality is likely to have played a major part in the downturn.

The club secretary mentioned that she had worked at the Fonterra plant at Edendale until she lost her job when they shifted their operations to Mosgiel.

'I was a director of the Southland Dairy Co-op in the years leading up to the merger with Alpine,' I told her. 'Must have been twenty years ago.'

'I was working there at that time,' she said. 'Knew the names of every milk supplier then, but it's too big for that now.'

She filled my water bottle and I left this heart-warming business, walking down the lane past a herd of settled Jersey cows that watched me with large amber eyes. As I headed upstream I thought about the human scale of Retro Organics, and the close connection between the land, the cheesemaking plant, and the consumers of their cheeses — it's an operation that I sensed people could develop an affinity with, in contrast to the industrial-scale production visible on the other side of the river. What we have in the south is a landscape dominated by large-scale dairy farms where most of the milk produced is processed in Fonterra's gigantic plant. The end products leave Southland by train and ship, heading to the far reaches of the planet. The Fonterra approach — characterised by world-scale, low-cost commodity production — has required a massive growth in milk volumes, leading to an ever-growing footprint of dairy farms on the land. I fear that the rising nitrate levels in the groundwater and rivers, as a result of this expansion, risk becoming our own version of Silent Spring.

Further upstream I could see the curving cliff on the far bank where I experienced a memorable day on the river close to sixty years earlier. It was the first time I had fished downstream of Mataura. I was taken south by Mr and Mrs Cunningham who lived two houses up the rise from us in East Gore. They had come to New Zealand from Scotland. He was short, stout and most of the time wore overalls that smelt of the grain and fertiliser that he handled every working day; she was as small as a bird. I was a regular visitor to their little house where they spoke gently to me in the accent of their home while I sat at their kitchen table eating Mrs Cunningham's scones and reading the *Beano* comics their family sent over from Scotland. Once in a while Mr Cunningham would let me look at the fishing flies he kept in a wallet made up of thin felt pages, each holding delicate little slope-winged flies, some attached to fine coils of nylon.

On the day we drove south I sat between them on the warm engine cover of the Bedford truck Mr Cunningham drove for his job as a storeman in Gore. At the river I hurled my worms into the deep hole beneath the cliff and sat on the bank with Mrs Cunningham while Scotty (as I called him later, when I was old enough for it not to sound rude) headed off downstream swinging his little wet flies through the rippling water.

That afternoon I landed three trout from the same deep hole. They were bigger than I had seen before and convinced me for a time that the further from Gore I could get, the bigger would be the trout. While exploring the riverbank close to my rod I saw two black eyes looking up from the muddy bottom of a backwater. When I stood over them I could make out the faint outline of a flat fish. I still remember the excitement I felt as I lowered my hands, at first slowly, and then with a lunge, at the outer edges of the fish. It turned out to be a large flounder, almost black-backed, and writhing with the shock of it all. Mrs Cunningham found it hard to believe that such a fish could be so far from the sea. It went into my fishing bag along with the trout.

Scotty arrived back at the end of the afternoon without a fish, complaining that the river was full of waste from the freezing works, and threatening not to come back. He looked less pleased at my catch than I expected.

At home in East Gore the fish floated stiffly in our laundry tub. Dad weighed them on Mum's kitchen scales — the biggest was four and a quarter pounds, and the other two just under four. He rubbed his face red with excitement. 'Three big trout and a flounder, caught by a kid. I'll ring the *Ensign* — this is a real story,' he said, although I doubt that he did call them because I never heard from a reporter.

***

I followed another looping bend of the river, crossing under more electric fences, before leaving the paddocks to track upstream on the road to an anglers' access a couple of kilometres downstream from the steaming chimney of a wood-processing plant. The path to the river was overgrown with long summer grass nodding in the westerly breeze. Because this is one of the few anglers' access points on the true left side of the river between Wyndham and Mataura, I expected to find vehicles and anglers ahead of me, but I had the place to myself.

The course of the river here is directed by the eroded seams of rock that cross the valley. The flow initially left a long flat, accelerated through a narrow chute where it built enough pace to throw up some white water, before regaining its composure while it sidled past a couple of small islands. Willows lined the far bank, but on my side there was a beach mostly made up of smooth, fist-sized stones. I waded into the current that had taken on the colour of the blue sky and turned over stones to get a fix on the health of the river. Many mahogany-coloured mayfly nymphs darted for cover, while stony cased caddis larvae occupied many of the nooks and crannies on the stones, their jewel-like homes made of tiny pebbles and sticks of various shades held together by silk secreted from these creatures that spend most of their lives hidden from view.

My gas stove made short work of boiling some river water, before I added half my daily allowance of ground coffee and lay in the long grass to read more of Laurie Lee's adventures in Spain while savouring the smell of the brewing coffee.

Towering cumulus clouds marched over the landscape from the west, bright and white on top where they billowed towards the sun but shredded and grey underneath, speaking of storms to come. I drank my coffee and ate chunks of cheese from the block of Mataura Tasty. It felt good to be eating it on the banks of the river just a few kilometres from where it was made.

The Hokonui Hills, which three days earlier had looked a world away, now sat clear and close, a mix of tussock and remnant forest just twenty kilometres to the north-west.

During the first days of my walk I heard little from the river, the sounds from its lazy flow lost to the wind, but in this spot, with just a breeze blowing, the sound of the boisterous river was my background music.

Mayflies started to hatch and flew without test flights or

instruction on delicate wings towards the willows and long grass. I strolled up the beach hoping to see trout feeding on the mayflies in the shallows, but none was visible. Hundreds of empty nymph shucks left behind by the mayfly duns floated amongst the stones — a reminder not of a death, but an old life let go in favour of a short future spent above the surface of the river. In a day or two the duns would shed their outer skin and once more return to the river to mate in an aerial dance over the smooth flow above the ripples before depositing their eggs on the surface, their life's work complete.

Upstream the flash of sun from a fly rod caught my attention. The angler stood in a thigh-deep glide that I have fished many times, mostly during the autumn when the afternoon mayfly hatches can be stunning. On the best of those days I have spent afternoons surrounded by so many rising trout that I didn't feel the need to move more than a few metres.

Before heading north I opened my Topo map to check the distance to Mataura. Just six kilometres to go — not much more than an hour and a half, I thought. Maps have captivated me for a long time, and the detail on this 1:50,000 map gave it a three-dimensional feel. The orange-coloured roads depicted on the western side of the river had a spoke-like symmetry, with Mataura township at the centre, while those on the eastern side were without pattern as they followed streams and bushy ridges across the map, like the veins on the face of a heavy drinker.

Back at the road, while I waited for a car to pass, I was surprised to hear someone say, 'Hello.' It took a moment to locate the person who spoke, looking up at me from the long roadside grass.

'Hi. Were you the guy I saw fishing upstream?' I said.

'That's right. Had a great session. You missed a nice hatch — plenty of fish about. The ones I landed were all over three,' he said with disarming honesty, referring to a place some might have been less open about.

'Great stretch,' I said. 'I've had so many good days here but don't come so often now. My fishing base is in Balfour. Usually stick to the upper river.'

'You weren't fishing when I saw you?'

'No, I'm walking up the river from Fortrose to the source in the mountains. Well, that's the plan, anyway.'

'Really? Good on you. Pity we didn't meet yesterday. We could have put you up near Wyndham. We're doing up the old doctor's residence down that way. Actually, my wife enjoys doing things up, and I like the fishing. Dunedin's home though,' he said with a chuckle. 'You know Witherow? He's in Balfour, I think. He's responsible for getting David Murray-Orr into flying.'

'I've fished with Dave for over forty years,' I said, 'and shared a place in Balfour with him for a long time.'

'My wife gave me a day's guided fishing with David Murray-Orr as a present. It's a gift that truly keeps giving. He showed me some fine places to fish, and spending time with him changed the way I fish. I'm fishing smaller, lighter flies than before I met him,' he said.

He pulled himself out of the grass to shake hands. Tufts of greying hair pushed out from under his hat, as though he had an old dog trapped under it, and his lean face was etched with a warm smile. We said our goodbyes when his wife arrived to collect him, and I turned north towards Mataura and my rendezvous with Sue.

A couple of kilometres upstream I reached Tuturau, and the tired-looking roadside reserve that commemorates the battle that took place there in 1837. Ngāti Tama warriors from the Nelson area travelled down the West Coast, crossed the Haast Pass, and came south in the hope of capturing the Murihiku land of the Mataura. In their book *The Sorrow and the Pride: New Zealand war memorials*, Chris Maclean and Jock Phillips describe the battle that took place on the site as being more of a scuffle than a real battle. The village at Tuturau was taken by

Te Pūoho and his warriors from the north, but three days later he was shot and the village retaken by warriors from Ngāi Tahu, and Tūhawaiki, the Ngāi Tahu chief, who had travelled from Ruapuke Island. Maclean and Phillips note that the obelisk to mark the events that took place at Tuturau carries an inscription in English which doesn't mention Ngāi Tahu or Ngāti Tama and reads as if it marked the mainland triumph in an inter-island rugby match: 'The last fight between North and South Island Māori in which the southerners were victorious took place in this locality in 1836.'

Beside the river near Tuturau I found a sign declaring that the next few kilometres of river, extending just beyond the Mataura Falls, to be a mātaitai reserve inside which the taking of short- and long-finned eels and kanakana (lamprey) was prohibited.

Bob McDowall described in his *New Zealand Freshwater Fishes: a natural history and guide* the importance of this river fishery to the early Māori. They travelled to the area seasonally to harvest eels which were especially important to their wellbeing because they were large, abundant and easily caught. Māori also established a temporary village at the base of the Mataura Falls, a place described by early residents of Mataura as 'the fish market', to harvest kanakana. McDowall described their method of gathering the lamprey: they would fix stout poles into holes alongside the falls and use these to lean out and pluck the kanakana off the rock face. Once caught the kanakana were sometimes stored alive in corfs in streams handy to settlements. They were also dried on racks by wind and sun.

The arrival of the European settlers didn't harm the kanakana fishery at first. In 1901 the *Mataura Ensign* reported 'the Mataura Falls is pronounced the best fishery in the colony'. The good fortune didn't last long. In 1905 the same paper reported that, 'owing to the increase in pollution of the Mataura from mining operations kana-kana now practically ceased to run up the river, as was their wont from time immemorial'.

With the establishment of the paper mill on the eastern bank of the falls in the 1870s and the meat plant on the western side in 1893, the emasculation of the falls (Te Au Nui, the great swift current) was complete, and the kanakana fishery a shadow of what it was.

The establishment of the mātaitai felt like a very small sign of hope in what has been a grim treatment of the river — especially this part of it, which was important to Māori.

The architecture of the river changes near Tuturau. Over thousands of years the river has carved itself a deep channel through a band of sandstone that crosses the valley here. It is the only section of the Mataura that is constrained by rock walls, but because there is little gradient it flows deep and slow, threaded with seams of white foam that snake across its surface. The first gold found in Southland was taken from this part of the river. In the late 1850s a group of Europeans spent a couple of months extracting gold from the area, but eventually left after enduring bad weather and finding only small quantities of the metal.

Frigid rain lashed me as I walked into the bleak southern outskirts of Mataura township. A couple of long black American cars from the sixties sat incongruously on the edge of the road outside a sagging wooden bungalow. Large dogs eyed me from behind a fence that looked incapable of holding them back had they decided they didn't like the look of this bedraggled stranger walking into town. It was only four in the afternoon but the grey light and rain-slick streets made it feel later.

A little further along the footpath three surly-eyed youths ambled towards me, smiling in a smart-arsed way when they forced me to leave the path to get past them. The encounter left me feeling discouraged for their future prospects rather than any sense of anger.

I looked at the river from the concrete single-span bridge at Mataura. I've always found it a forbidding, gloomy structure, but was pleasantly surprised by the view below because for the first time I can recall I could see the stony bottom through the deep, pale green water. I've got history here, not all of it good, but it reminds me of how attitudes to the river have changed, mostly for the better. Back in the 1960s, I sometimes threw the contents of a rubbish drum from the bridge into the river. When I was growing up my Uncle Ray had a bookstore on Main Street, just half a block from the river, and I worked for him a couple of times in my school holidays: my time in the shop with my uncle played a part in my love for books, even though the range of books for sale was limited by the small market. Looking back, it was a modest shop, but I loved it — the people who came in to pick up their weekly magazines, the smell of the books. Most of all I relished the chance to talk books with my uncle. One of my early morning jobs was to take the rubbish to the river. I wasn't alone doing this, which now seems unspeakable: most of the local shopkeepers did the same thing, as though the river existed to take away rubbish. The river smelt bad then. A few hundred metres upstream of the bridge a series of pipes disgorged blood and all manner of stinking animal waste from the freezing works, along with the odd load of discarded paper pulp from the paper mill. It is little wonder that the shopkeepers saw no reason to treat the river with respect because its desecration had already taken place.

A few years later, after leaving university I returned to the south where for eighteen months I had a job at the mill. Some lunchtimes I would eat sandwiches on the rocks overlooking the falls and watch trout fling themselves at the wall of rock. Opposite my seat on the rocks, pipes belched blood, fat and animal waste into the river. Bloated eels and trout, and hundreds of gulls, gorged on the stinking protein. The river, which entered the falls mostly untarnished, left the area fetid and dirty.

This day, as I looked north towards the now inoperative paper mill, and the freezing works where the majority of the discharge has been stopped, the river looked cleaner than at any time since I first looked upstream from the bridge over fifty years ago.

On my way to the Falls Hotel, where Sue had booked us a room for the night, I walked down Main Street, which was a shadow of the busy place I recalled as a teenager. Some of the shops were boarded up, and I struggled to recognise the façade of Uncle Ray's old shop.

The entrance to the Falls Hotel wasn't encouraging: a sign on the door warned that people wearing gang patches and insignia weren't welcome. It reminded me that during the time I worked in Mataura I never went inside the hotel because of its unsavoury reputation and the sense I had that going in there wearing a suit would be as wise as going into the bush wearing a set of antlers. However, the greeting from the couple who managed the hotel was friendly. Settled into our modest room I eased off my boots, checked my heels which had held up well, fell onto the soft bed, and waited for Sue. The cold, bleak entry to the town was quickly forgotten as I relaxed, elated to have completed about a third of the walk, and excited at having Sue on her way. From here on I would be walking into more familiar territory. The place where I was born and grew up was just half a day's walk upstream. Beyond there the river becomes unchecked by the tight confines of its banks, allowing it to roam more like a braided river. Best of all, within a day I would have rounded the Hokonui Hills and started walking towards the mountains of northern Southland.

Sue told me the news from home while I washed away the day's dirt and sweat in the shower. Nothing much had happened except that Izzy, our much-loved feisty dog, had required more pills to keep her going.

'I feel like a walk through town,' said Sue. It wasn't high on my list of things to do, but I had been doing what I wanted these last few days — and besides, our two Westies deserved a walk after the long ride in the car, so off we went. Mataura has lost a quarter of its population since I first knew it, and it showed in the number of uncared-for houses, some with battered old cars on what years ago might have been front lawn but now looked like unkempt paddock. Interspersed with the dilapidated houses were a few with manicured lawns, tightly clipped shrubs, pristine paint jobs, and not a thing out of place, as though their occupants were making a stand against the decline around them.

Back at the hotel, when we entered the bar for a drink we were stared at as though we had forgotten to put on clothes, but our novelty soon wore off. We ate an oversized meal of fish and chips in the hotel restaurant, busy with a friendly Friday-night crowd; mostly families with children running about having fun, and older couples dressed up for a night out. It felt like a scene plucked straight out of the 1980s, as though the last thirty years had still to arrive.

A couple stood under cones of light thrown from poles in the vast car park. They weren't far apart, but stared off in different directions, like the disconnected figures in a painting. After an hour of sleep, I woke to the sound of men's voices, thick and rough, and the high-pitched laugh of a woman, followed by the throb from a V8 leaving the car park at speed. My night was dream-tossed, mostly nightmares involving my little tent, perched on the side of an abyss, in complete darkness. When I woke my pyjamas felt glued to my body by cold sweat, my head throbbed and my stomach grumbled. I downed a Panadol, fell back on the bed and watched the light slowly fill our room.

Sue had brought fresh supplies with her: nuts; energy bars; dried meals; cereal; and, vitally, more coffee. I had failed to measure the supplies out into meal-sized packs the previous night, and when I finally got out of bed to try, my head swam and I couldn't concentrate on the task. I lay back on the bed feeling listless and despondent.

'You need a good coffee. That café on Main Street might be open,' said Sue.

'Not a chance. It's not even eight,' I said gloomily.

'I'll drive to Gore, then. Bound to find something there.'

While she was away I contemplated my options. The thought of spending a day in a bed at the Falls Hotel felt like a nightmare, and while going back to Dunedin with Sue was probably the sensible decision, it smacked of giving up, just when the prospect of completing the walk was becoming a reality.

The coffee Sue found in Gore, and the power of the Panadol, gave me enough energy to get my food sorted. I wasn't up for breakfast, but I did put the muffin Sue got me into a handy place in the pack in case I felt ready for it. Our two dogs sensed action and stood at the door, tails vibrating with an excitement I couldn't feel.

I sent a text message to my cousin Tracy who lived close to Gore, near my planned route on the eastern side of the river, to ask if there would be a bed at his house in the event I couldn't carry on.

MATAURA TO GORE

'Why don't you come back to Dunedin with me?' said Sue. 'You can start again when you feel better.'

I sensed she was right, but felt a desperation to continue this journey, even though the reasons for the walk had been blurred by the waves of nausea that swept over me. I knew I wanted to write a personal memoir of the river as it was now, and what it has meant to me, but something else was pushing me past my sickness and weary legs. Perhaps a fear of failure was at the heart of it. For a couple of years the thought of undertaking the river walk had become more important to me than I was prepared to admit, even to myself. Backsliding now didn't feel like an option.

We stood on the side of the rain-slicked road a few hundred metres north of the bridge, holding on to each other, before I stepped back and tried to smile into Sue's camera. 'Looking good,' she said, with a look on her face of hope rather than truth. Knut stared at me through the back window of the car as they headed away, his coal-black eyes looking at me with an uncertainty that echoed mine.

My plan for the day was to walk north on River Road, on the eastern side of the river, to Gore. My legs didn't feel up to staying on the riverbank, but I knew the Mataura would be in view, close to the road, most of the way. Beyond Gore I planned to follow the riverbank and camp near Knapdale, in the lee of the Hokonui Hills.

On that damp cold morning, walking between the now-redundant paper mill (in 1876 it missed being the first paper-maker in New Zealand by just one month) and the misty hills in the east, Mataura felt a depressing place. Originally called 'The Falls', and later taking the name of the river that flowed through it, I reflected on the part this town has played in desecrating the river. Just a few metres west, beyond the dank walls of the paper mill, lay the most impressive natural feature on the river — the Mataura Falls, hidden from close inspection for over a hundred years now, its spray and sound lost in a tangle of buildings.

I made better progress than I had imagined possible when I started the day. Initially the road ran beside the river, and a couple of kilometres upstream of the town boundary I pushed through the willows and stood on the bank. The river here isn't compressed by sandstone walls and consequently runs wide and shallow. The stony bottom was visible as far as the opposite bank, perhaps sixty metres away. A few mayfly duns hatched into the misty air, and along the quiet edge where the current idled over algae-stained stones mayfly spinners, delicate wings flattened to the water, drifted downstream in their funeral procession. Trout rose nearby, unchallenged by anglers.

My heart lifted when I looked north to catch my first glimpse of the Umbrella Mountains beyond the Waimea Plains, but eventually my lack of breakfast and queasy stomach took its toll. The focus of my walk narrowed, and I counted progress one telegraph pole at time. Eventually I took off my pack, leaned on a farm gate and ate my muffin watched by hundreds of sheep. Under dry leaf litter at the base of a shelter belt I lay back on my pack; closed my eyes; and, accompanied by the sound of sheep sniffing and snorting as they edged towards me, waited for the sugary energy of the muffin to kick in. The curious sheep closed to within ten metres, watching me edgily, before bounding off at my slightest movement.

After making a recovery of sorts under the trees, I headed north, into a part of the river rich with meaning for me. Just upstream, near where the road and the river converge, I caught my first trout on a summer outing with my family. I'm told I was four at the time, so it must have been the summer of 1953. We didn't own a car, so I imagine we went there squeezed into Uncle Ernie and Aunty Ngaire's Chevrolet, because they were with us. No photographs exist of that afternoon on the river, so the vivid memory I have of much of what took place is untainted by some reconstruction of the truth based on images looked at decades later. The feel of the worm in my fingers as I slid it onto the hook, the steep and narrow gravel beach, the jerking of the rod tip, the pull of the trout, and the fish lying beside me on the gravel remain real to me, so potent was the experience. My memory of the day isn't perfect, though, because at the time I felt we had travelled a long way south of Gore. As I sat beside the river in the place where I thought we were that day, it was clear from the map that we were just a few kilometres from the town.

Beyond the intersection with Diamond Peak Road a car passed me slowly, before pulling up ahead. My cousin Tracy climbed out. 'Hi, Dougal. How are you? Did you get my text about a bed at our place?'

'Gidday, Tracy. I didn't — I turned my phone off. I should be okay, though. This bug feels like it's just holding off,' I replied.

'Why don't I take your pack on to Gore? You can decide from there what you want to do.'

'Wow, that would help me along. Should make Gore in a bit under an hour if that works for you.'

'I'll look out for you at the bridge in about an hour,' he said.

Close to the southern edge of Gore, where the river runs

through another series of water-sculpted sandstone and seams of lignite I scanned the opposite bank trying to identify the place where, when I was eight, I gaffed eels with Morrie and Jessie Corrie.

On the southern outskirts of Gore I found the spot where my Uncle Bonner once had an odorous factory where animal parts were boiled in vats to extract fat. The building no longer stands, but I thought that I could make out where it used to be. It was there, one summer Saturday morning in 1957 or '58, that I walked down to the river by myself while Dad talked with his brother. I cast my little metal lure at a trout that finned in the current under a veranda of willows. I remember the thick, humid air that smelt of summer grass, boiled animals and the sewage that flowed into the river nearby. I recall an image of the trout I found hovering close to the surface, and the willows dipping the tips of their branches into the river, and my amazement when it eventually grabbed the lure, only four or five paces from me, and the startled look of the trout after its fatal mistake. Determined not to let it go I walked backwards, towing it onto the grassy bank where it lay while my heart thudded in my skinny chest. It was the first trout I had landed while fishing on my own. With a couple of fingers firmly inserted behind the trout's gills, I ran over the paddocks, arriving breathlessly in front of Dad and my uncle, holding the trout out as though I was making them an offering. I insisted on Mum cooking it, even though it came from an undesirable part of the river.

***

Soon after I crossed the Waikaka Stream I met Tracy walking towards me. He had left his car in Gore and walked back to join me for the final kilometre into town. 'You know, I've lived on Diamond Peak Road for years and I must have driven this road thousands of times, but this is the first time I've walked it,' he said.

I was born in Gore only a few blocks from the bridge we approached. For almost all of the years I lived there as a boy, I hadn't thought about living anywhere else. My parents, brothers, sister, grandparents, uncles, aunties, cousins, all lived within a short bike ride from my home in Wentworth Street. Only Tracy and one other cousin remain living in the area. I don't see much of him these days but because we are family, and about the same age, I find it easy to pick up the threads of our lives. He is starting his fifth term as mayor of the district.

'Five terms — that's impressive. I think our great-grandfather David McDougall was mayor for about as long. You two have done your bit for the family,' I said.

We stopped part way over the bridge into town and looked down at the river, braided, clear and low. It's a bridge I must have biked and walked over thousands of times in the years before I went to university. Some years I looked into it so often I believe I knew every place that held a trout.

'The river's looking great; sure better without the sewage that floated past here when I was a boy,' I said. 'Mind you, when I looked off the bridge back in the sixties I always saw plenty of trout. I've only seen one today.'

'Can you remember throwing the rubbish from Dad's shop into the river off the Mataura bridge?' asked Tracy.

'I can. You know, I've been thinking a lot about that these last few days. How attitudes to the river have changed. Can't imagine it happening now.' I leaned on the railing of the bridge, waiting for a wave of nausea that gripped my stomach to pass.

'Why don't you call me when you get to your camping spot tonight,' said Tracy. 'I'm more than happy to drop your pack up to you.'

'That would be a huge help. Not sure I would make it if I had to carry it,' I said, lifting my forehead from the bridge railing.

Thirsty and drained of energy, I headed for the Capri Café on Main Street, hoping that a milkshake might give me enough strength to cover the eight kilometres north of Gore to my destination by the river near Knapdale.

**

I was fortunate to grow up in Gore. The hills I raced my trolley down and wandered over with friends, bird-nesting and digging up rabbit holes, were close, as were the streams and river that captured me from the start.

Looking back at my early life I realised I had a limited sense of what Gore was like before I knew it. I imagined its past as a black-and-white version of the place I lived in. I don't recall being taught the history of the area, and the reading I did as a child wasn't about places like Gore — little of it was about New Zealand. The worlds of Robin Hood, Daniel Boone and Davy Crockett, king of the wild frontier, felt real to me in a way that early Gore didn't.

Before my walk I spent time in the Hocken in Dunedin, trying to get a sense of what the river and its catchment might have looked like before the arrival of the Scots and English colonists. There I found the writing of James Herries Beattie. He interviewed the few Māori living at Tuturau to try to get as 'close to the truth as we shall ever know' of the place before the colonists. He noted that the place where Gore now stands was largely an area of swamp and lagoons, interspersed with rushes and stands of cabbage trees and mānuka. Blind Creek ran where Main Street is now. He reported that in 1858, when Thomas MacGibbon camped near the Mataura at what is now Gore, he described the river as a 'clear, silvery pellucid stream'. There was, according to MacGibbon, 'nothing but solitude, unbroken save by the plaintive cry of the quail or the shrill croak of the weka'.

The pace of change in this late-settled landscape has been extraordinary. When I was born in Gore, just one long lifetime after MacGibbon camped beside the river, little remained of the largely untouched land he described. Few of the indigenous birds were able to adapt to the removal of the native vegetation; the draining of the land; and the introduction of rats, cats, dogs, stoats, ferrets, weasels and rabbits, along with a Noah's Ark-load of exotic birds. The native quail went early, followed later by the whio (blue duck). The brown teal disappeared and black teal numbers fell; I never got to see a kingfisher there, described as once being common in the district. Sadly, my mind was too muddled with the poor state of my stomach to think of much of this as I trudged down Main Street to the café.

***

At the Capri I ordered a milkshake, and sat with my map spread out on the table while I contemplated my route north. A wave of nausea hit me soon after the milkshake reached my stomach. I looked for a sign to the toilet, but for a moment felt so weak that I feared I would fall over if I attempted to stand. I slumped forward on the table and tried to steady the world that had started to spin. My shirt clung to my body and sweat beaded on my forehead while I wrestled with my options. Reluctantly I decided that trying to walk upstream during the afternoon wasn't one of them. I thought about taking Tracy up on his offer of a bed, but wanted to be by myself and didn't want to ask Sue to come back from Dunedin to get me. The place I use as a fishing base in Balfour, a couple of days' walk north but less than half an hour's drive, was where I decided I needed to be. There, I thought, I could hide away in silence, like a sick dog, and wait on the bug to pass.

I called Dave in Balfour. We have fished together for over forty years, and for close to twenty owned a fishing base in the town with JD, another long-time fishing friend. Dave has his own place there now, and because he was recovering from a broken leg, I guessed he would be at home rather than on the river.

'No problem,' he said. 'I need some supplies from Gore anyway. See you outside the New World in forty minutes.'

Tracy dropped off my pack, and a short time later I was headed north with Dave. 'Come round for dinner if you're up to it,' he said when he dropped me off.

'Thanks, but I can't imagine eating a thing.'

Inside I threw off my clothes as I walked to the bedroom, grabbed a Panadol and slid under the duvet. My dreams were so vivid and disturbing that I spent the afternoon unsure whether I was asleep or awake in some awful new reality. My body alternated between being goose-bump cold and so sweaty that my sheets were soaked.

I lay in the black night, and reached out for something to hold on to. The sound of the river was close, and I felt wet from the flow which tugged at the tent, threatening to take me downstream. In my panic I fumbled with the tent zip that wouldn't open. When I woke I felt for a moment like a little boy in the bedroom I shared with my brothers in Gore, so scared of a ghost standing in our wardrobe door that I couldn't move. My heart pounded on, minutes after I worked out where I was — alone, in a dark Balfour bedroom.

I slept until after nine the following morning. The fever had gone, but I was deeply tired and decided I needed a day of rest. I spent the morning sitting on my deck, feet up, finishing off Laurie Lee's book. Once again, the reality of my walk felt different from the glamour of his adventure. He wrote of exotic food and the erotic pleasures enjoyed by a young man in Spain, while all I could think about were my cracked heels, weary body, and the dismal Southland summer that had lashed me as I walked upstream. While I had planned to camp beside the river most of the time, I reluctantly decided to use Balfour as a base while I crossed the Waimea Plains. Without a tent and food my pack would be lighter allowing me to cover the ground more easily than before, and I hoped the evening conversation in

Balfour would lift my spirits. JD, who had just arrived in Balfour for a few days of fishing, agreed to help me with the logistics by following me while I left my Balfour-based Land Rover where I planned to finish for the day, before driving me south to the place where my walk had finished the previous day.

GORE TO DILLON ROAD

I leaned into the nor'wester that blew like a banshee across the Waimea Plains and wondered what the hell I was doing as I watched JD drive away after dropping me on the northern outskirts of Gore. My old Land Rover was parked beside the river at Dillon Road, twenty-five kilometres upstream, and I feared that my body, still recovering from whatever it was that struck me down two days earlier, might not be strong enough to get me there. Ahead of me, rows of wind-sculpted clouds hung across the sky, their white leading edges as smooth as an aeroplane wing, while on the lee side they were grey and ragged.

When I was a boy I worm-fished the river where my walk for the day started, lobbing my bait into the deep slow pools, close to the indentations left by the mechanical buckets that took gravel from the river. As those buckets were dragged across the river they left behind water-filled dredge holes as big as tennis courts, where trout cruised close to the steep gravel banks. Once in a while, after securing my rod on a willow stick, I would lie on the edge of a gravel bank with my Brownie camera and click off a roll of black-and-white film at cruising trout. The results were mostly terrible, with just the odd shadow of a trout visible under the reflection of the sun that bounced off the water to spoil the image.

One Saturday afternoon I walked the area with an older friend who owned a .22 rifle and, after not finding any rabbits, watched wide-eyed as he managed to stun a trout by holding the barrel under the surface and firing as it cruised past. I remember urging him to do it, and then being horrified when the trout floated, white belly up, to the surface. We walked back home to Wentworth Street, terrified that someone would spot us carrying a rifle, a trout and no fishing rod.

I followed the river on the eastern bank through land converted from sheep to dairy farming in the last few decades. The landscape here is dominated by the mass of the Hokonui Hills, which were just visible in the north when I began my walk on the coast. They appeared to be real mountains when I was a boy, but smaller now as my horizons have expanded. The remnant forest on their eastern flanks looked almost black under the cloud shadow. It was the first significant piece of largely unmodified landscape I had been close to since leaving the coast.

About four kilometres upstream I looked for an area I had fished back in the fifties with my friend Jimmy. On some spring weekends we biked halfway to Knapdale to fish, hunt for birds' nests, dig up rabbit holes, and set fire to the odd gorse bush. The look of the land had changed so much since my time there as a boy that I wasn't able to recognise our old haunts. A series of creeks had run across the paddocks when we explored the area then, and in one of them, under a wooden bridge, I found a broad-headed fish with gold spots on an olive body. At the time, it was just another fish to marvel at, but it was almost certainly a Giant Kokopu, or native trout. Often, when I crossed the bridge, I would lie on the rough planking and slowly push my head over the edge to look into the water. The fish, which was the size of a small trout, was well camouflaged among the water plants swaying in the current, but if I waited long enough I could usually find it. Once, I dangled a worm in front of its blunt nose but it rejected my offering. It was there for just one spring, and the following year I wasn't able to find it. Fifty years later the creeks that once flowed through this land have mostly been turned into sterile channels or run hidden through tile drains. Discouraged by the changes, I sat and ate an energy bar while the wind battered the seed-heavy grass as though an invisible pack of dogs was tearing over the land.

I was pleased to be walking away from the lowlands, towards the Mataura Range flanking the Nokomai Gorge and, on the Umbrella Mountains, the last of the high snow that feeds the Waikaia River, the Mataura's largest tributary. There is something about this high country at the northern edge of the plains that lifts me — snow-covered and crystal-sharp in winter, tawny and untamed in summer. One of the benefits of not fishing while I walked was the freedom it gave me to move with my head up, looking at the way the wind, clouds and angle of the sun changed the texture of the land.

I looked back towards Gore and the hill on the northern edge of the town on which the water-tower looked out over the valley like a medieval fort — and the cemetery which lay on the slopes below. My chest heaved with an involuntary gasp as I thought about walking away from my family buried on that hill. Dad was forty-one when we left him there, my brother John just twenty-seven, and my baby sister Sally. My Gran and Pop Hicks who were close to the centre of my boyhood lie there, as do uncles, aunties, cousins and great-grandparents. They all left an imprint on me, but the impact of Dad's death has been the most enduring. In the months leading up to his stroke he and I found much to argue about. Mostly it was about rugby and the shortcomings he saw in the way I played, but the clash of expectations went deeper. We stopped talking to each other for close to a week during the worst of our differences. A few years earlier such insolence from me would have ended with a hiding, but I had reached an age when that wasn't an option, so we fumed at each other, neither of us knowing what was happening to him at the time — that the headaches that left him grey-faced with pain were the symptoms of the slow blockage in his brain that would eventually end his life. He wasn't himself, and I was just a teenager, too self-absorbed to see it.

In the months that followed his death I gave up the sports that I loved, studied hard for the first time, and took over our vegetable garden where he had left off. I suspect that my changed behaviour was partially driven by guilt, and while I'm mostly over the trauma of it, decades later it can surface to occasionally send me spinning. There was also perhaps a desire in me to show that we could go on functioning as a family, as though nothing had changed. My grandfather tried to help with the gardening, but I resented his kind hand because I needed to show I was good enough to keep us going.

I don't expect to join my deceased family on that hillside, but I take comfort from knowing that is where their journey ended, on the slopes overlooking the river and mountains.

Upstream of Monaghan Road I walked a stretch I often fished with Uncle Ernie back in the 1970s. The river, wide and mostly shallow, curved out of the north-east, largely as I remembered it. It was easy to imagine my uncle walking beside me with his short bandy legs, Skellerup thigh-waders, a roll-your-own smoke stuck to his lip, and his worker's duncher on top of his slicked-down hair. I remembered the frosty early starts and those times late in the morning before we headed back to Gore, sitting on the banks of the river eating Aunty Ngaire's Belgian biscuits while we talked about fishing and our lives.

Near where the Mataura curves back to almost touch Knapdale Road, I clambered through the willows and ate a nectarine beside the water. Here the river flows over eroded formations of rock that cross the current at right angles.

Sheltered from the wind, I could hear the river song as it cascaded through the reefs. The rock is part of a massive fold of land pushed up millions of years ago as two tectonic plates were squeezed during the formation of the Southland syncline. The uplift, which looks like the ridges on the back of a tuatara, runs east from the Takitimu Mountains to the Catlins coast. This part of the uplift was initially sliced by the glaciers that pushed through the area intermittently over hundreds of thousands of years, before being worn down by the thunderous flows that followed. Lake Wakatipu once drained down this valley, as did water from the Oreti catchment.

Between the rock seams near Knapdale and the Otama bridge, almost two hours' walk west, the river flowed through a series of lazy curves between low grassy banks and shingle beaches. From the southern edge of the Waimea Plains all the way to Cattle Flat the river becomes braided, mostly unconstrained by the push of hills and the solidity of rock and lignite. These days it is the section of the river I know best. The walking felt easy, partly because I had left my tent and most of my food in Balfour, where I planned to return for the evening. The broad gravel fans at the downstream ends of the pools were easily crossed, enabling me to walk from beach to beach, avoiding some of the tangled vegetation that had slowed me below Gore. I often spooked trout from the shallow gravel edges. I also found them suspended in the current where the fast, ripply water dropped into deep runs.

The northern ridges of the Hokonui Hills rose like ramparts on my left as I walked towards Mandeville — into a land drier in the rain shadow of this first significant barrier faced by the storms that roll off the Southern Ocean. When I was a boy the high ridges of the hills were cloaked in native bush and the lower slopes were dense with tussock, but much of the tussock and some of the bush has been removed in the last few years, killed off by spray, and replaced on the fragile slopes by pasture.

As I walked on I felt saddened that the look of this landscape, visible from much of northern Southland, could be modified as though the aesthetics of the land counted for nothing. Since the fires in the thirteenth and fourteenth centuries that destroyed much of the lowland forest which once covered the area, tussock has held the land together, reducing the run-off during heavy rain and delaying the drying of the land during droughts. The alteration of the landscape by the first European settlers might be understood but the clearances that go on today are without excuse — because the consequences are known.

***

Approaching the Otama bridge I had a powerful memory of swimming in the area when I was perhaps seven. We were there as a family on a warm afternoon, rugs laid out on the gravel. Dad sat in the flow so that I could climb up his hairy back before he would stand and stagger into deeper water. I held onto his head while balancing on his shoulders, looking at the rushing water, willing myself to jump, before leaping into the roiling current. Emboldened, I leapt again and again, pushing further out each time, while Dad rubbed his face red with excitement.

When I was around twelve I camped by the river near Mandeville with the Boy Scouts. We pitched our tents under willows in a farmer's paddock and spent a couple of days exploring the riverbanks, lighting fires, cooking and throwing stones at seagulls. During the second day someone discovered that the mince for our evening meal, which had been hanging in a muslin bag from a willow branch, was fly-blown. Our leader said that the meat would be all right to eat because the eggs hadn't hatched. They did, though, need to be removed so I was sent to the river with a couple of mates to wash them from the mince. Soon after we dipped the bag into a back eddy of current and began brushing the eggs from the muslin, an eel slipped out from under the bank and swam towards the berley trail of mince juice and fly eggs. It was one of the largest eels I had seen. When we lifted the mince from the water the eel turned its attention to the metal milk container sitting in the water. We watched, enthralled, as it scraped at the metal with its teeth, its fat body writhing like a snake's.

A summer or two later the *Mataura Ensign* reported that a man swimming in the river at Mandeville had been bitten 'on the big toe' by a large eel. The head of the eel was cut from its body, and the man was taken to Gore hospital to have its inward-curving teeth removed from his 'toe'. It took me a day or two to understand why Mum and Dad thought this was funny, and that the big toe referred to in the *Ensign* was his penis. It left me wondering if it was the same eel we saw at the Scout camp.

***

Early in the afternoon I lay on the bank a few hundred metres upstream of the Otama bridge, weary from the long walk in the gale and the lingering impact of the stomach bug. I had lunch, removed my lightweight wading shoes, shook out the accumulated gravel, took off my socks and massaged my feet.

The Otamita Stream entered the Mataura a few hundred metres north of my lunch stop. I have a photograph of me swimming in a pool on the Otamita. I'm in the water with my sister, two brothers and two other girls. It was a couple of years after Dad died and before Mum married the father of the girls we swam with, making us a family of nine. Initially the union added an optimistic note to my life, something I thought might help overcome my sadness, but watching Mum fall in love with another man simply added to my sense of loss. The fractures created continue to run through our lives, like ripples radiating from a rock thrown into a deep pool.

I first fished the stream in the spring of 1977. That day the Otamita was flanked by steep hills covered with the red tussock that likely would have surrounded the men who entered the valley in 1869 to release trout into the stream. They were the first trout released into the Mataura catchment, and played a part in creating one of the finest brown trout fisheries anywhere. Until the late 1990s I thought the Otamita was the perfect early-season trout stream. It bounced its way towards the Mataura over a stable bottom rich with mayflies, caddis, dobsonflies, koura and snails; the trout were heavy-shouldered and generally larger than their counterparts in the Mataura. It cleared quickly after floods and its flow held up during the dry summers because, almost magically, the tussock extracted moisture from the clouds that piled up on the hills, even when it wasn't raining, releasing it into the peaty ground which in turn nourished the stream. My heart wasn't captured by the wonders of the water cycle — I fell instead for the hefty trout, the tussock-softened hills, the hatches of mayflies and the boisterous flow. The tumble of water that grabs at the air, taking it deep, before releasing it in lines of bubbles along the folds of current. It reminded me of the stream that ran through my favourite pre-school book, *Scuffy the Tugboat*.

The tussock is now mostly gone, and the essence of the stream has changed, leaving it just a shadow of what it was. The Otamita, along with most of the Mataura system, was the subject of a water conservation order in 1997. While the order might have made it more difficult to dam the flows of the waters, and tightened up on discharges allowed into them, it had nothing to say regarding protection of the catchments, so critical to the health of the Mataura and its tributaries. In the twenty years following the conservation order, the catchment of the Otamita has been changed beyond recognition, and its once outstanding fisheries values have been decimated. Cattle now graze pasture on land that, when the order was passed, was still covered in tussock. They have been allowed to wander at will in the stream, eating the last of the native flax and breaking down the fragile banks in the process. Environment Southland knew what was happening, because I and others told them, but either they were powerless to act or their priorities lay elsewhere. There might still be days when the Otamita fishes well, but I rarely go there now because once it was extraordinary, and I find its deterioration difficult to confront.

A couple of kilometres upstream, in the lee of wind-thrashed willows, swallows plucked mayflies from the gale and, where a long ripple dropped into a deep pool, three large trout levitated in the current. I crossed the river where it curved out of the east, and among a heavy growth of willows found the unpromising confluence with the Waimea Stream. The Waimea's modest flow left the weedy avenue it pushed through the willows to be lost in the Mataura as though it never existed. It begins as a creek draining the Lintley Range east of Lumsden, remaining tiny until a series of springs close to Balfour add to its flow. Back in the 1960s the Southland Catchment Board decided that its meandering course over the plains was an inefficient way of draining the land, so it was given an engineering make-over. Many of its curves, along with much of the stream-side vegetation, was removed, and the Waimea was cut off from some of the wetlands that succoured it during dry months. It was treated as though being a drain was its main purpose. The stream has carved a modest valley on the western edge of the Waimea Plains, all manicured paddocks now, shelter belts and a thread of willows marking its course. It is as pretty as a picture, as are the mountains in the north. A viewer could be forgiven for thinking that nothing much has changed, so timeless is the scene — but the reality is different. Within fifty years of the first settlers arriving most of the tussock had been cleared, changing the look of the landscape, and around a hundred years after their arrival the Waimea was seen as an inconvenience that needed to be put in its place.

It took at least a couple of decades for the Waimea to recover from the channel straightening. In places it has recaptured some of its curving form, and willows have regrown to hold the banks and provide shade from the sun. The populations of snails, caddis flies and mayflies have recovered, as have the trout and eels that rely on them. Most who farm the valley have fenced stock out of the stream and in places have begun to restore native plants along its banks.

For the last fifteen years the Waimea has been my local water, being just a few kilometres west of our place in Balfour. In the spring and early summer, before low flows and smothering weed make it difficult to fish, it provides challenging fly-fishing for large, extravagantly spotted trout. I've had some magical days on the Waimea, but I fear for its future — nitrate levels in the water have been rising yearly and are unsustainably high, threatening to choke it with excessive plant and algae growth.

My legs ran out of bounce during the last hour and I checked my map several times, hoping the next curve in the river would lead me to the hillocks of gravel that marked my destination for the day. Around five, after close to seven hours' walking, I reached the Land Rover at the end of Dillon Road. I hadn't seen another person on the river in the twenty-five kilometres covered, and looked forward to a meal, some conversation and a good bed.

DILLON ROAD TO
WAIPOUNAMU

Next morning JD dropped me back to Dillon Road around twenty kilometres south of my destination at the Waipounamu bridge. My walk upstream was into a landscape I knew intimately from decades of walking the river with a fly rod, looking for trout. This part of the river felt like one of my old Beatles records, played so many times that I knew what note came next. I bounced along, knowing that by the end of the day I would have reached the halfway point of the walk to the headwaters. Grey shredded clouds were powered over the plains by a westerly gale, but I was buoyed by the small patches of blue that threw a patchwork of optimistic light over the mountains in the north.

I didn't bother to cross the river to find the place Fortune Creek enters the Mataura. The slow destruction of this once-magical spring creek is, like the decline of the Otamita, almost too much to bear. For two decades I fished Fortune Creek for the trout that finned in its crystal water. It was so intimate that I learned more about approaching trout with stealth than anywhere, because if I wasn't careful the trout didn't give me a chance. Nothing much was caught by accident in Fortune Creek. On my Topo map it looked like any number of creeks that threaded their way to the Mataura: it didn't reveal its true beauty until you found it and took half a day quietly walking up its banks, taking it all in. When I first came across it, I was reminded of the fabled spring creeks I had read of in Hampshire. It would have been at least their equal, with its rich fly-life and numerous trout of up to five pounds.

Beyond the Fortune Creek confluence I walked up the long bank from which I hooked and lost the largest trout I have seen in the Mataura. That day, around thirty years ago, I cast my tiny nymph at what for a time I thought was probably a branch lying in the calf-deep water. There was a surreal quality about the evening — a kind of perfection about the light and the still-warm air that didn't feel real at the time. The branch was so large and dark that it didn't look much like a trout, so my first casts at it were practice shots, unfurled without any expectation of the target being a trout, but something held me there, casting until the branch moved a fraction in the direction of my nymph. On my next cast it shifted gently in the flow as it swallowed the nymph. It didn't run far or fight spectacularly, and in no time I was walking along the bank with the trout holding in the current a couple of rod-lengths away, as though it was a dog being taken for a walk. There were few obstructions nearby, and I started to feel a confidence that this great trout was going to be mine. When it was just a rod-length from the bank I could see a plume of blood pulsing from its gill plates like a Lancaster bomber billowing smoke from a shot-up engine, and I felt it was only a matter of time before the fish would give up. Alarmingly, though, it resisted my attempts to roll it ashore. Glancing downstream I spotted a single gnarly willow on what had been, when I first looked, a bank free of all apparent danger. While the willow was new to me, I sensed that the trout knew exactly where it was, as it inexorably worked its way downstream. Eventually we reached the willow and the hole that had formed around it. The trout dropped over the lip into the deeper water a few metres above the willow and, close to safety, turned its head down and used its big tail to drive it towards the tangle of roots. I gripped the line against the rod, turning the trout onto its massive side, before the tippet broke and the fish drifted without righting itself into the willow. For a few moments I wondered if the experience had been real. And why I had been so mesmerised by the trout that I hadn't been tougher on it earlier. The fish, which I was connected to for perhaps quarter of an hour, must have been well over ten pounds — improbably large for the area, and too large to have been sitting in the shallow water half a step from the bank. Except it had been there, that summer evening. By the time I reached the car, the disappointment of losing the fish was replaced by a sadness at the waste of it all, because the trout bled so vigorously that I doubted it would survive.

***

Trout fed along the shallow edge of a pool dimpled by light rain as I reached the open banks near McAllan Road. Upstream, a guy who I assumed to be a guide hovered like an anxious parent behind his three clients who cast flies towards the willows. The clients looked conspicuous with their fancy hats, new-looking clothes and tentative wading, as though they weren't sure of the bottom. One of them eventually hooked a fish which was lost when the guide swooped his net towards it. With the fish lost I walked towards the guide, who approached me with the look of someone who was getting ready to deal with something unpleasant.

'I don't have a rod,' I said and his face relaxed. 'I'll stay back from the bank and cross way above your guys. Where are you based?'

'I'm out of Nokomai. Down here to dodge the gales,' he said with a chuckle.

'Hope you have a good day,' I said as I headed upstream, crossing to the western bank half a kilometre above the cluster of anglers. Part way across I stopped to watch four trout jostle in the knee-deep current while they fed on nymphs and the odd dun.

After three hours of easy walking I reached my lunch spot opposite a quarry half a kilometre downstream of the Pyramid bridge. The westerly gale had gone, replaced by a light drift from the south. In the still air I could smell the river again and the herbal aroma from the desiccated grass, dampened by recent light rain. While I snacked on sardines, creamy duns hatched and drifted on the light air. Downstream two trout rose steadily in a line of foam that marked the snaking conjunction of currents. Without competition from the blustery gale I could hear the rustle of the river as I leaned into the gravel bank and looked south towards the serrated ridges of the Hokonui Hills.

After lunch I lifted the pack onto my back and pushed north towards the bridge, cursing the precariously small gap between the electric fence and the river. Jersey cows followed me so closely that I could have touched their moist noses, had I not feared losing my balance in the process and toppling down the steep bank into the river.

The lull in the wind didn't last, and by the time I approached the confluence of the Mataura and Waikaia it once again blasted at me from the west. I sheltered in the lee of a high bank beside a stretch of water Dave had named Morsie's Ripple, after an Australian friend who landed untold numbers of trout there one day a couple of years earlier.

Out of the wind I munched on an energy bar and thought about a day on that ripple the previous season. That day I hooked half a dozen trout in the first thirty metres on a tiny dry fly, while Dave struggled to find fish on the other side. 'What are they taking?' he yelled across the flow in a tone that showed he wasn't getting any pleasure out of watching me hooked up.

He eventually landed a couple near the head of the ripple before he departed upriver. When I reached the Waikaia confluence I could see him, rod bent into a trout. There was no point both of us fishing up the Waikaia so I carried on up the Mataura. Late in the afternoon I leaned back on one of the Alaskan bush tyres on his little aeroplane, enjoying the warmth of the sun while I waited on his return. Dave doesn't wear a watch or carry a phone, so his grip on the time is tenuous. When the fishing is going well he is reliably late — sometimes worryingly so. There was just enough light left for our flight back to Balfour when I saw him crossing the river towards me. His jaunty stride, beaming face and the lateness of the hour told me all I needed to know about how his day had gone.

'Best day I've had in years,' he said. 'Fish everywhere, and mostly big. Nice hatch got going — those big dark mayflies. Brilliant.'

'Mine was good too, but not that good.'

There isn't much middle ground with Dave. This is as true with his fishing as it is with his life. If the weather is bad or the fishing not to his liking he turns despondent and grumpy. He would rather lie back with a good book than put up with a poor day on the river. It takes just two or three days of fishing that he considers to be substandard for him to declare that the river's stuffed, and that he might 'give up this fucking game'. But when it's good the dark days are forgotten, and he can't stop smiling at his good fortune.

***

I tried to take a photograph of myself standing with the two rivers joining in the background. I put the pack on the gravel, sat my little camera on top, set the timer and quickly took up a position in front of the colliding water. Before the shutter clicked open the wind blew the camera over, leaving it to take a blurred close-up of my pack. After a couple of failed attempts,

I propped the camera up on some stones in the lee of my pack and finally got a shot of me pointing back at the confluence. It's mostly a photograph of stones with me leaning into the wind. The modest-looking water in the background of the photograph gives no hint of it being a place where these two fine trout rivers join.

The Waikaia drops steeply out of its sources in the Garvie and Umbrella mountains before unfurling its way down a valley just fifty kilometres long. Perhaps because of the short journey it takes from its mountain source it usually feels colder than the Mataura, and it might be the higher oxygen content of the cold Waikaia water that makes the fish there feel as if they fight harder than do trout from the Mataura. The two rivers carry a different hue — the Waikaia peaty-coloured, like a much-diluted whisky, and the Mataura almost colourless but for a hint of blue, like the palest of blue eyes. Their base material is also different — smooth, worn gravel and stones in various shades of grey in the Mataura, while the bottom of the Waikaia comprises stones that are darker, many of them rough-edged, like fractured schist.

Upstream of the confluence the Mataura was as low as it gets. Dry, cool westerly winds had pummelled the lower South Island for a month, ruining summer holidays and leaving the land bone-dry because most of the moisture in the air fell as rain on the western side of the alps, leaving little to make it to this inland plain. I had lived in the south long enough to know these conditions were unlikely to last, and the previous night in Balfour I heard a weather forecast for the following seven days foreshadowing a massive low-pressure system sliding south-east over the Tasman Sea. A weather bomb was mentioned, with the prospect of extreme rainfall over parts of the south. I worried about what it might mean for my walk, particularly the section in the Nokomai Gorge two days' travel upstream, which might become impassable if the river rose.

It might have just been a trick of the light, but when I looked north the Mataura Range looked much closer than it was when the day started, and the hills that flanked the eastern side of the river fell away behind me as I pushed further north onto the alluvial plain. The land was flat, apart from the old river terraces sliced into the land thousands of years earlier. The plains, once covered by forest and tussock before the arrival of humans, are now a mosaic of pasture grasses and shelter belts, crisscrossed by long straight roads. There were patches of remnant forest nearer the coast, but here on the plains I didn't see even a token of its existence.

The combination of the low river and numerous gravel beaches allowed me to cross the river with ease and dodge the lines of willows that often flanked one side, or the other. Under the wind-torn surface of the ripples I saw trout swaying in the current as they hunted down food. Some of the creamy duns that hatched were taken by trout, a few caught in the tumbling air by terns, and the rest swept off in the gale. Tucked in the lee of the willows a couple of large trout pushed unhurried bow-waves upstream as they sucked tiny willow grubs from the surface film.

A couple of kilometres downstream of the bridge near Riversdale I came across a herd of dairy cows wandering along the riverbank. Closer to the coast I had seen cows on the banks where they had pushed through inadequate fencing — but here there was no sign of a fence.

It was close to five in the afternoon when I reached the bridge near Waipounamu, feeling strong, as though I could have walked on for another couple of hours, but my Land Rover waited for me under the bridge so I threw my gear on board and headed to Balfour.

In Riversdale I leaned on the Land Rover outside the dairy and sucked down my banana milkshake, while on a nearby bench a couple of Aussie fishermen licked ice creams, looking flattened after what must have been a tough day in the wind. From the fragments of conversation I overheard, I gathered that they had hardly seen a fish all day. While I had seen plenty, I had covered over twenty kilometres and knew that even if I had been carrying a rod, trying to fly fish in the gale would have been a challenge.

That evening Ray and Denise joined us for dinner at Dave's place. They farm mostly sheep near Cattle Flat on a property that shares a long boundary with the Mataura. Their family is so steeped in the district that the bridge over the river at Ardlussa carries the name of Ray's forebears.

There is nothing fancy about the meals we cook in Balfour, but they are mostly delicious. Dave's meal was no exception — slow-cooked lamb that fell apart at the lightest touch, crisply roasted potatoes and parsnips, carrots and peas, with gravy and mint sauce. Just what I needed after a long day on the river. The other unexceptional thing that happened was a lively conversation about the state of the world — falling apart, according to Dave — and the river: the talk was helped along by wine and a few single malts. While I recounted stories about the difficulty I found walking up the riverbank, particularly when I was closer to the coast where the tangle of rank vegetation between the river and electric fences made walking beside the river almost impossible, Ray talked of the issues they sometimes have with anglers roaming over their property. 'The other day some clown parked by one of our gates, climbed into the paddock without asking, and from the look of his bloody tracks I could see that he had walked right across a newly sprouted winter crop,' he said. 'These guys that can't be bothered to ask just piss me off.'

We first met Ray through aviation. A few years back Dave saw me on the river while he was flying upstream looking for a place to fish. He landed nearby and strolled over to see how I was going, and while we were talking another microlight circled over us before it too landed beside the river. The pilot turned out to be Ray. Over the years Ray and Denise have become our friends, and generously allow us to cross their farm to get to the river, as they have allowed others to walk through designated anglers' access points.

'Too many abused the privilege, though,' said Ray. 'Walked in, even when we had closed access temporarily because of crops or stock. In the end we decided just to close the place off. Even the local cop used to ask permission — opened the season at our place for years. Used to take the police car down to the river where he left it on the flood-bank, with the door open so he could hear the radio. Plonked himself down in his uniform, and spent the opening morning worm-fishing.'

'World would be a better place if more cops took up fishing,' said Dave, his face glowing from the warmth of the single malts and the heat from his diesel fire — even though this was supposed to be the middle of summer.

'Call in at our place for morning tea when you walk past,' said Ray as they were leaving.

'Will do. Should be there in two days if the weather behaves.'

It might have been the whisky, but when I lay in bed I thought that my well-walked body felt better than it had for years. I was exhilarated to be past halfway, and desperately hoped that the weather would allow me to keep going.

WAIPOUNAMU TO SHEEPWASH CREEK

By six I was awake and restless to be walking again, on what I expected to be my last day on the Waimea Plains. In the seventeen years I have shared ownership of the Balfour house with Dave and JD, the majority of our fishing on the Mataura has taken place where the river crosses this alluvial plain. The area feels like old New Zealand. The population of the district, from Gore in the south to Lumsden in the north, hasn't grown in my lifetime. The removal of most agricultural subsidies in the mid-1970s hit the district hard. Sheep numbers declined, and the new economics of sheep farming meant a reduction in the number of workers that could be supported by each farm. For around twenty-five years the population in the area shrank, and school rolls declined. House prices became decoupled from the lift in values in the large urban areas while shops, banks and stock-and-station agents closed; some pubs closed while a few struggled on. The more recent growth in dairy farming has stemmed the population decline, breathed new life into the rural economy and the school roll in Balfour is increasing again, but the cost of the change can be measured in declining water quality.

I showered with the bathroom door wide open so that I could hear the start of *Morning Report* on the radio. The walk had so consumed my thinking that the news that floated into the bathroom might as well have happened on another planet. When the weather forecast began I leaned out from the steamy bathroom to listen. A deep low was approaching the West Coast, and heavy rain and high winds were forecast for much of the South Island. Extreme weather alerts piled up. Damn it, I thought. This is February, usually dry and settled. What's going on?

Breakfast consisted of two highly coloured farm eggs on grainy toast with baked beans and bacon strips on the side. I suspected I would need all of that to get me through the day.

JD called in for a brew of coffee, and we talked of our plans for the day. 'Don't like that forecast,' he said. 'I'll drop you off and head home. I'm not fishing in that.'

I left the Land Rover near the river where I expected my walk for the day to end, midway between Tomogalak Stream and the prosaically named Sheepwash Creek that runs from the southern end of the Mataura Range. Soon after nine, JD drove us down the rough track beside the Otago Anglers hut by the Waipounamu bridge. We stood under a sky that looked like newly poured concrete and joked about the last time we used the hut in the days before we had our property in Balfour. 'Remember that guy we shared the hut with?' I said. 'He's one of the few people I've met through fishing I haven't liked.'

'The one with the married girlfriend. So excited her husband was away he ran into the ditch when he took off to see her,' said JD.

'That's him. I think booze put him in the ditch,' I said. 'Didn't think about it at the time, but we shouldn't have helped him. He would've been a menace on the road.'

'Heard him arrive back around sunrise. Still snoring in his car when we left to fish,' said JD.

***

I headed upstream on the eastern bank and spent the following twenty minutes stumbling and cursing my way through a tangle of willows strewn with flood debris before eventually making it to open, dry sheep country and long gravel beaches. The river had risen slightly and carried a blue mist after overnight rain in the headwaters. It rolled south in a series of broad sweeps, leaving nothing more than a murmur in the still air. A couple of skylarks sang above me as they climbed on their near-vertical path above the dry grass. The plains opened ahead, while in the south the Hokonui Hills appeared to shrink, as though being swallowed by the land.

An hour upstream I saw an angler, one of fewer than half a dozen encountered in over a hundred kilometres. Under a mizzle of rain I sat on the bank eating an apple while I watched him, his rod flexing in the cast before the line was unleashed in a narrow unfolding loop towards a trout that fed close to a scrawl of willows — those alien trees, here in a place where not one existed just 150 years ago. They, along with many other species introduced here by the settlers, are a resilient lot. The willows, mice, rats, trout, mallards and other introduced creatures and plants have an evolutionary toughness, stemming perhaps from the array of threats they adapted to on the Eurasian land-mass — something lacked by the endemic grayling, kiwi, falcon and other creatures and plants that were either forced into isolated pockets or driven to extinction.

Eventually the trout pushed a bow-wave upstream, unimpressed by the delivery of the fly, and the angler waded over for a chat. Like the majority of the people I see on the river these days, he looked to be in his sixties, lean and fit.

'It's been a slow day,' he said in a North American accent.

'Tumbling air pressure from that storm won't be helping.'

'I'm hoping it won't wreck my walk. I've walked up from the coast. Just past the halfway mark. Where are you from?'

'Canada. Come here each year, partly to dodge some of our winter, and the fishing's usually great — but this year the weather's been bad. Perhaps I should have stayed at home,' he said with a wry smile.

'I've lived here a long time, and I don't recall a summer like it,' I said.

As I walked upstream I reflected on how few people I was seeing near the river, and how those I was seeing were mostly like the Canadian and me — retired white men, most of whom got into fishing when the world was different for young people. These days I can easily go a season without seeing a teenager on the river.

A lack of damaging floods through the winter and spring left the bottom of the river stable, with a fine glaze of periphyton on the stones. The shape and position of the ripples and pools appeared largely unchanged from the previous autumn. This is not always the case in this part of the river. Across the plains the river has few hills or rocky structures directing its course, and consequently it wanders across the flat land, regularly cutting new routes through the light soils. While the mayflies and caddis that make up the majority of a trout's diet have evolved in tandem with the river, there are times, after heavy floods, when the density of bottom fauna is reduced. The trout population can fall sharply in those years, and the fishing suffers accordingly. It is often a month or two into a new season before we find the stable sections that have moved least.

Despite the instability of the river on the plains, it has become the area I have fished most these last twenty years: partly because it is close and we have got to know it well, but also because the angling pressure is mostly low. I also find beauty in the often dry land under a big sky, framed in the north by mountains that rise out of the flat land into snowy crags.

My progress upstream was rapid, broken each hour by a quick stop for food. When I started the walk I imagined that during these stops I would lie back in the grass with sun on my face while I contemplated the scene, but sadly those days were rare. On this day the wind that was building out of the north-west carried a cold edge and the sky remained depressingly leaden. I walked on with my rain jacket zipped up and my hat secured by a chin strap to stop it flying off. The mountains in the north looked grim and implacable under caps of grey orographic cloud, and the surface of the river looked opaque and metallic under the reflection of it all.

For an hour or so I walked beside a part of the river I knew first in the mid-1960s, soon after Dad died. My girlfriend at the time lived with her parents on Waipounamu Road, just a few paddocks east of my track beside the river. It was a time when I needed to hold and be held more than I understood, because while I was part of a loving family there weren't many hugs going in our lapsed-Presbyterian household. We often sat for hours outside her house in the front seats of Mum's Morris Minor, condensation building on the windows, holding each other with the innocence most of us had back then. Once in a while we crossed the paddocks behind her parents' farm worker's bungalow and walked by the river. Solid trout lay close into the banks behind clumps of sod that had toppled into the flow then as they do now.

An hour downstream from Keowns Bridge I met a fly fisher from Tasmania who, like the Canadian earlier, was in the area for a month. He said he had deserted his home waters because the insect life in them had been ruined by pesticides used on crops entering the streams. 'The Mataura looks in great shape. Plenty of fish about, and the bottom looks clean,' he said. 'Don't like the look of the weather, though.'

When I mentioned that I had a fishing base in Balfour he

looked at me with a hint of caution in his eyes. 'You're not David Witherow?'

'I'm not, but it's a small world down here. He's been a close angling mate for years.'

'He's established quite a name for himself. Doesn't like foreign anglers at all,' he said.

'He's got some strong views on the subject. Claims not to like Aussie anglers in general, but I've got to say, he knows a few at a personal level, and gets on famously with them.'

I left him and waded to the eastern side for the last push to Keowns Bridge, only to be confronted by another three-wire electric fence. Because I couldn't squeeze under the lowest wire I had to shuffle along the narrow strip between the wires and a rat's nest of willow and flood debris. In the time it took to scramble my way to the bridge hard rain had started to fall and a southerly front sent the temperature plummeting. Pigeons burst away as I clambered under the bridge to shelter from the rain. A quick measure of my map showed that the Land Rover was still about six kilometres upstream. There are times when I enjoy walking in the rain but on this gloomy day I wanted to end the walk as soon as I could, so decided to push on without any further breaks, thinking that if I hurried it would take about an hour to reach the vehicle.

Swales and densely packed willows pushed me off the western bank so I crossed the river to be confronted by a couple of kilometres of thigh-high wet grass. In what looked like a new farming experiment the large paddocks had been sliced into a series of tiny lots, each one surrounded by an electric fence. I felt as though I was walking through a bath of custard, and my legs were dead by the time I extracted myself, crossed the river yet again and found a paddock of grass, munched mercifully low by sheep.

A Cessna 185 slid past at low level, headed north under a layer of grey that slanted towards the horizon, before landing on a farm strip a short distance upstream. I presumed it was going to ground before the rapidly approaching storm eliminated the prospect of safe flying.

There is a solid population of good trout north of Keowns Bridge but on that bleak afternoon I didn't see one until I came to a deep hole formed where the first hint of the high country squeezed against the river from the east. A fish that looked about five pounds sidled along the edge of a deep hole where the old river channel butted against a rock wall. There is no scientific evidence to support the claim that trout and, more important, the insects they feed on can detect changes in the weather before they occur. However, on this day, the visual evidence suggested the trout were aware of an approaching storm, and had laid up in deep water.

The Tomogalak Stream was dry where it normally ran into the Mataura. A couple of months earlier I had taken a few fat trout in it, but they were a long way apart. It is a delightful stream, which anglers who don't measure the quality of the day by the number of trout landed might cherish.

**

Back in the 1970s I came close to losing my life on this section of the Mataura. I was canoeing downstream from Parawa through the Nokomai Gorge with my brother-in-law Geoff, and in a benign section of the river, near where we were expecting to be picked up, we were forced off course and tangled with willows. Before we were able to correct our line in the slow-turning Canadian canoe we were thrown towards a stout, sawn-off willow branch that lay horizontally over the water at about the height of our canoe. Geoff, who was up front, dropped backwards into the canoe moments before our prow slipped under the branch. I was at the back, using my pack for support. The pack stopped me from lying back so I was left to duck forward, the branch knocking my hat off, before slamming into the pack. The canoe stopped as though someone had applied the brakes, and for a moment the current threatened to sink us. Just as the water began to surge over the back, the canoe dipped enough to release it from the grip of the branch. Later, when I opened the pack, I realised how fortunate I had been. The combination aluminium billy-and-bowl set at the top of the pack was heavily stoved in where the branch had slammed into it. My head had been just a couple of finger measures below the point of impact.

That day we were to be picked up by our wives where a footbridge crossed the river. Unbeknown to us the bridge had been washed away a year or so earlier, and while we saw our ride throwing dust off the road just a hundred metres away, and I stood uncertainly in the canoe throwing my arms about, our wives didn't see us.

When we passed the confluence with the Tomogalak Stream I knew we had gone beyond where the bridge should have been, so we pulled the canoe out at a beach and walked over some paddocks to the closest house, where we hoped to call our family in Gore. It was the Saturday of my youngest brother's twenty-first birthday party, and we were expected in Gore to celebrate the affair. When the farmer came to the door he was happy for us to use their phone, but they had a party going on for a reason I no longer recall, and insisted, since we had canoed down the river, that we first join them for a drink and some food. This we did, and before long the afternoon was slipping pleasantly by. They had a helicopter out back, and when someone suggested that we might like to take a flight with them I thought things were getting out of hand, and we should make the call. An hour later when my stepfather picked us up we were pretty well lit up by the hospitality that had been showered on us. Back in Gore we were deeply unpopular, and it was long into the night before some would even speak to me.

***

I trudged the last couple of kilometres beyond the Tomogalak soaked from the waist down, water streaming off the brim of my hat. The rising country on either side of the valley was obscured by a dirty sky. When I reached the Land Rover, my drenched jacket, sodden trousers, and the last of my body heat steamed the windscreen. Outside, the feeble wipers flailed hopelessly at the driving rain.

Back in Balfour for what I hoped would be the last time on this walk I ran a bath, threw off my wet clothes, broke off a chunk of peanut slab, poured a solid vodka, stared briefly into my tired-looking face in the bathroom mirror, and climbed into the steaming water. The vodka went down in a gulp, the chocolate more slowly, as I sank up to my neck listening to the staccato rain on the iron roof. Sometime later I woke to the sound of voices, followed by Dave's head appearing around the bathroom door. 'I'm off to Paul Eaton's shout with Greg. His son's wife has just had a baby. How about coming with us?' he said, retreating rapidly to the dining room.

'You sure? Don't feel I know Paul that well,' I called out.

'Don't be silly. We checked with him. It's no problem.'

I dodged the dark puddles in the car park before entering the cavernous building now used as a workshop. It had housed Balfour Motors in its heyday. For a time in the sixties more Fordson tractors were sold from this place than any other Ford dealership in the South Island. The business failed decades ago, and the building has stood beside the main highway as a sombre monument to the change that swept away much of the old order of rural New Zealand. It's now a prominent and ugly blot on the landscape, and probably creates a bad impression of Balfour for motorists speeding to and from the Southern Lakes. That suits my angling friends fine, because we like the place as it is — quiet, and mostly forgotten by the busy world.

Despite the warmth from a couple of diesel-fired heaters, it felt almost as cold inside the building as out. Forty or fifty people, a sizeable portion of the population of the district, stood around eating sausages, beef patties, onions, lamb chops and steak, all cooked indoors on a couple of barbecues. A blue haze from burnt diesel and sizzling meat hung in the air. The guests, mostly men with pale foreheads above tanned faces and a small number of women, stood around high tables while children played around the dark fringes. The men mostly drank Speights and clutched meat sandwiches in their work-tough hands. There were no speeches, just much talk and celebration for the birth of a child. It was, like most of the people who live in the district, an unpretentious and friendly affair.

The rain that fell on the asbestos roof sent rivulets down the outside of the windows; condensation fogged the insides. My legs felt heavy and tired as I stood on the concrete floor, which had a patina of oil and fuel stains. In the gloomy corners of the building were benches piled with tools, and parts of old vehicles in various states of assembly.

I talked with Ron, a dairy farmer with a property in the Waimea Valley, about my walk. 'And what do you think of the river?' he asked.

'In some ways the Mataura looks as good now as I can recall,' I replied. 'It runs clear and the bottom is clean, even downstream of Mataura, where it was in bad shape when I first knew it. Turned over plenty of stones, and mostly thought the insect life was healthy. The few fishermen I met also thought it was in fine shape.'

His faced brightened, as though he had been braced for a different message. 'Really? You need to go and talk to Environment Southland. They think it's in a bad way. You know, I'm sick and tired of hearing people on the radio, most of them living in Auckland, bagging dairy farmers. I've lost all respect for them. They have no idea what's going on in the country. I care about the environment and have a pride in my farm and my stock. Most dairy farmers are doing their best to look after the environment. I'm pissed off that these people think we are all like the few who don't care.'

'In terms of fencing stock from the river,' I said, 'I think you're right. So far I've seen just a few examples of stock getting into the river. It's the leaching of nitrogen and phosphorus into the groundwater that's the issue. It's slowly choking the small streams with weed. Eventually it'll damage the Mataura. It's the pace and scale of the dairy expansion in the south that's been the problem. Most individual farmers look like they are trying to do the right thing, but the overall impact is a problem.'

I finished my beer, ate a steak sandwich, and looked across the room for Greg and Dave. The cold concrete had chilled my feet, so I decided it was time to return to my unit and pack for the next day.

Christmas lights — red, yellow and blue — swayed in the wind above the wet street as I headed west. Through the window of the cavernous pub I saw a couple of men sitting at a table with a jug of beer between them, the otherwise empty space giving off an air of despair. Rain swirled around the street lights but nothing much else moved along the broad road.

Back at the unit I filled zip-lock bags with three days' supply of breakfast and lunch snacks, chose a few dried meals, and stuffed them all into my pack. My tent topped the load off, with my sleeping bag in a water-tight bag in the bottom compartment.

Anxious dreams punctuated my sleep and I woke with my T-shirt clinging wet and my sheet damp, as though I was sleeping in the tropics. In the pre-dawn dark I listened for rain on the roof, but heard none. I thought that I might have been lucky and that the weather bomb had passed. When I emerged from the shower the news from the radio wasn't good: a band of heavy rain was forecast, along with damaging winds that were predicted to exceed 100 kilometres an hour. Outside in the pale early light I could see puddles on the drive but the rain that fell wasn't much more than a drizzle, and the wind just a whisper. I wondered for a moment if I was standing in the quiet eye of the storm.

The weak cellphone signal didn't kick in until I reached the street, and when it did the news was dismal. Environment Southland's webpage showed the Mataura at Parawa — upstream of my present location — to be rising steeply, up from eleven cumecs the day before to over fifty with no sign of the line on the graph topping out.

For a time I pored over the map of my route, looking for options to get through the Nokomai Gorge in such a flow. While it looked possible to follow the western bank without crossing the river, the high water would eventually force me to deviate over a saddle at the northern end of the gorge to avoid steep terrain beside the river. I was desperate to go on, fearing that a break in the walk might destroy the integrity of the journey. From past experience I knew it was unlikely that the river would fall and clear inside a week, and I didn't want to spend the last days walking beside it while it was high and discoloured. I called Sue to tell her I was heading back to Dunedin to wait out the flood, and trudged back to the unit feeling an empty despair.

My Land Rover doesn't have a heater, and even if it did the gaps around the doors and windows would suck any heat away, so I pulled on long johns, wrapped up as though for winter, and began the slow, noisy ride to Dunedin. By the time I reached Gore the wind and rain which threatened to overcome the sloppy steering of the vehicle lent certainty to my decision to leave the river.

The Mataura continued to rise, and within days was thundering through Gore at a staggering 600 cumecs — thirty times its volume when I walked through the town. Waikaia was cut off, stock lost and fences swept away. It was two weeks before the river reached a level that allowed me to continue with the walk.

THE RESTART: SHEEPWASH CREEK

On 7 February the river fell to a level that would allow me through the Nokomai Gorge without fear of being washed away. I headed south with a new set of boots to replace my fishing boots which, while good for a day on the river, weren't designed to cover around twenty kilometres a day, day after day. In Balfour I had a meal with Dave and Rick, our peripatetic friend who had recently returned from New Orleans. Early the next morning Rick dropped me beside the river where my walk had been halted. 'Might see you tomorrow,' he said. 'I'm planning to fish near Parawa. I'll look out for you. Might walk with you on the final stretch to Athol.'

'I should be out of the gorge early afternoon,' I replied. 'Might have phone reception by then. Be great to catch up.'

For half an hour I followed the road, the willowed banks of the Mataura curving away to the east towards the tentative hills marking the end of the plains and the beginning of the Garvie Mountains. A cool southerly breeze piled clouds against the high country, but I knew from the forecast that the air pressure was rising and the day promised to be fine. A couple of paradise ducks honked, sheep baa-ed and the gravel crunched under my boots. Otherwise the land was quiet. My body felt relaxed and strong after the days of waiting and my pack creaked in rhythm with my stride as I headed north. Ahead, the Garvie Mountains to the east and the Mataura Range to the west looked to have been cleaved apart by the river as it pushed through the first truly rough country I had encountered since the wild south coast.

I first fished this part of the river over forty years ago. Then the land was mostly used for low-intensity sheep farming and some beef cattle, but in recent years dairy farming has pushed north onto some of the river flats. Towards the end of the previous season I fished the area adjacent to my current path with a friend, Bob Morton, from Scotland. We spent an afternoon mostly casting tiny mayfly dun imitations to big trout feeding along current lines flecked with white foam, close in to the willows that carried the early colours of autumn. The day was soft and still under the palest of blue skies, the river low and, because the snow in the high country was all but gone, as clear as vodka. The trout, driven by a deep instinct to be ready for the only event that really matters to them — spawning — fed aggressively, but without offering an ounce of forgiveness if the fly dragged fractionally on the slick surface. It's the kind of fishing Bob and I treasure. We managed to catch a good number each, getting as close to the fish as we dared, and threw little curves into the line as it was being delivered to stretch the distance the fly travelled without drag. At times I put in around fifty casts to individual trout, holding my breath momentarily as the dun imitation sailed close to the nose of the trout before it eventually took the fly. We hooked around half the fish we cast at. The rest either sank slowly out of view after a few failed presentations, or were in such difficult locations we knew our chances of hooking them were slim.

We ambled our way upstream, taking a break every hour or

so to sit back in the dry autumn grass on the riverbank eating chocolate and nuts, and talking about all manner of things — the sort of conversation that comes easily when the rush of the mind has been slowed by complete absorption in fishing, and the sound dominated by the river as it shuffled on its relentless path to the ocean. Mostly we talked about the Mataura, and what a rare thing it was — the combination of large wild fish, clear water, quality hatches of fly, and relatively few people. Bob looked upstream where the river tumbled over a ripple before it slowed into the deep pool. After a few moments of quiet he said, 'If I had to design the perfect trout pool, this would be it.'

On that day we saw just two other anglers. They came up behind us late in the day, ushered along by an Australian guide who walked near them like a mother hen shooing her chicks along. They stalled fifty metres below us, looking as though they weren't sure what to do next. Eventually they started to fish, making casts so long over the slick water that their chances of getting a fly near the mouth of a trout without drag were close to zero. Mind you, one wore a large cowboy hat so white that most trout in the vicinity would have seen him coming some distance back. I felt a guilty pleasure in landing a couple, one over four pounds, while they looked on.

There was a darker side to this otherwise perfect day. One pool and long ripple was spoiled by the intrusion of a couple of hundred dairy cows. Bob and I watched their hooves break down the banks as they walked past us to shit and piss in the river. It was the worst example I had seen in a year or so of cows getting into the water, and it took some of the gloss off the day.

'You wouldn't see this sort of thing happening in Scotland,' said Bob.

I tend to be defensive about criticism of our beautiful land but all I could say was, 'Bloody disgrace.'

After taking photographs of streams of urine and cow shit landing in the river I called Environment Southland, explained what I had seen and sent off the photos and a map reference as evidence. Their reply wasn't encouraging: while what happened wasn't best practice, it didn't violate their current district plan. 'Keep an eye on it, and let us know if it happens again.'

I said, 'What's the point if it's not against your current rules?'

***

Back on the walk, dogs barked as they bounced off the back of Ray's quad bike, circling me in the muddy yard before running off as soon as he said hi. He offered me a cup of tea, but I knew it was too early for him to have a break; anxious to cover more ground that morning I moved on. I followed the river up through the property farmed by Denise and Ray and headed towards Cattle Flat Station on the western side of the river and Glenlapa to the east. The Mataura rolled south, its flow almost back to normal after the flood, but it carried a milky hue, as though it was springtime again and snowmelt was adding its mark to the river. As a consequence, the riverbed was visible only in the shallows. This would make crossing more of a challenge, causing me to rely on my memory of the river to pick the right places to cross. I unhitched the clip on the front of my pack in case I toppled over, and crossed cautiously, feeling my way with my feet and the walking stick.

The high country closed in around the river as I approached the Nokomai Gorge, the plains replaced by narrow river flats. Fingers of beech forest reached down from the high valleys to the edge of the river. With the bush came the sound of native birds, the first I had heard since leaving the coast. The pace of the river changed: the increased gradient and narrowing of its course added urgency to the flow. The bed of the river altered also. The fine shifting gravels of the plains were mostly replaced by larger, rough-edged stones, newly torn from the steep slopes and tossed down the creeks that describe their entry into the Mataura with fans of rock and debris.

Soon after lunch I reached the cluster of little do-it-yourself holiday huts that mark Cattle Flat. They appeared empty but during the holidays they are used, mostly by Southlanders who appear to enjoy the solitude at the end of the road, without cell-phone reception, internet coverage, electric power or reticulated water. Along with the grouping of huts near Fortrose and the few scattered along the river on the road to Nokomai, they are the only settlements that use the river as their focus. The towns of Gore and Mataura have been built beside the river, but for the most part they turn their backs to it. I imagine it would be different if the riverbed and banks could be privately owned. World-class trout streams like the Mataura can, in some parts of the world, be privately owned, and where this happens the few who can afford to build their mansions by the water do so because they can exclude others from walking and fishing on their property. We owe a gratitude to our English and Scottish forebears who, based on their experience in their homelands, ensured that such things mostly don't happen here.

A few years earlier I called into one of the huts with Kevin Ireland, a friend who was down from Auckland for his twice-yearly fishing trip. At the end of that day my old Land Rover, which was parked at the end of the road, wouldn't start, and we walked to the huts hoping to find someone who might be able to help. The only people we found were two women from Invercargill, both perhaps in their eighties. Their husbands had died years before, but they told us they kept returning for the solitude and the memories. When we found the battery in their car wasn't able to turn over the motor in the Land Rover, one of them insisted on driving me to Balfour, a half-hour trip. While I was away the other woman made Kevin a cup of tea and fed him cakes and scones. We arrived back to find him looking deeply contented, warming in front of a wood stove, as they swapped stories about their lives.

Kevin has visited the Mataura for close to twenty years. He

charms and entertains us with his stories, cooks fine meals, and directs the selection of wine with a knowledge that comes from years of experience. He can rave like a revolutionary at the injustices he sees in the world, while all the time retaining warmth in his eyes. His voice is about as big as he is; deep, and laced with more laughter than I hear from anyone. He's into his eighties and still rejoices at every trout he lands, and when he loses one he's inclined to exclaim, 'Oh boy, you should have seen it — it was a monster.'

***

The cluster of huts at Cattle Flat marked the end of the road. My path continued upstream along the banks of the river, flanked by a narrow strip of flat land on which cattle and sheep grazed. Half an hour's walk upstream of the huts I reached a paddock of Hereford cows and three heavily muscled Simmental bulls. Cows don't worry me, and most bulls I have encountered near the river usually pay me little attention, but the three creamy giants blocking my path locked eyes on me and began to bellow. The electric fence keeping them out of the river was placed within a metre of the high bank, leaving me to scramble up the rough river edge, eventually passing within a few metres of the rippling bulls who watched me with a menacing disdain.

For a time I followed a rough farm track over a beech-covered spur. The air, which was cool in the shade of the trees, carried a tang of moss and leaf litter. While descending towards the narrowing valley floor I watched a large trout sipping insects from the foam-streaked surface of a backwater. If I had been carrying a rod I would have bent low, crept down the track to the valley floor then moved on my knees to get as close to the fish as I could before settling my fly into the foam — as I have done many times before in that exact spot. Instead, I sat on the edge of the track and watched the trout move lazily into the rotating current, feeling happy on that day at least to be leaving it alone. From my vantage point I could see the river bouncing off a rock wall on the western side of the valley, before turning west towards me.

Unlike most other great trout streams on the planet, the pools, runs and ripples of the Mataura don't have names that are widely used. Perhaps this is because the angling history of the river is short or it could be because as we walk less we have lost the need to build a picture of the land in our minds. Even among my angling friends we have few words used to describe places on the river, despite the importance of the Mataura to our lives. Ripples and glides, as well known to us as the back of our increasingly veined, sun-marked hands, are often referred to as, for example, 'that big ripple, half a kilometre down from the brown hut', or 'that glide under the high bank, just before you go over the second spur'. It's imprecise stuff. However, the ripple that lay before me as I sat beside the track above the sipping trout does have a name, known to perhaps half a dozen of my angling mates. Around thirty years ago I fished it with Randy Rummel, an American friend who was living in New Zealand at the time. That day he fished up the western bank while I worked my way up the opposite side. The ripple was busy with trout taking nymphs, and he landed thirteen in that one stretch. I christened the place Randy's Ripple, but because the name is only used by our group it is unlikely to outlast us.

The ripple running into the head of the pool above Randy's Ripple had, for a number of years, been one of my favourites, but the angle of the drop-off into the deep water had altered for the worse, and the food-producing stones on the bottom had been partially covered by fine gravel. I won't forget this ripple, because a few years back I fished it with Sue. She was new to fly-fishing but had landed several good trout during the morning, and, perhaps not understanding that bragging about how many you had caught wasn't how we played this game, gave JD a hard time about not landing as many as she had. 'Susie, that's not the done thing,' I said, grinning as we walked upstream. 'We try not to mention how many we caught — or if we do, it's a gentle, tentative thing.'

A storm moved in from the south that day. By the time we reached the area above Randy's Ripple a gale threw sleet at our backs, and snow had begun to settle in the tussock on the peaks. An armada of mayfly duns hatched on the wind-torn surface, drifted briefly, then launched themselves into the gale. Big browns scoffed them as they drifted, and in a short time I had landed half a dozen trout, most of which wore the darker, dramatic colours of spawning. I became so lost in the moment that I hadn't thought about where Sue was fishing. There was no sign of her as I glanced downstream. For ten minutes I thought she was probably enjoying the fishing around the corner behind me. After landing a couple more I reluctantly thought I had better race back and see how she was going. At the point my frustration at missing out on the hatch was turning to worry, I found her, huddled in between a couple of gorse bushes. 'Big hatch on, you've gotta get into them,' I said, before seeing that the colour had drained from her face, and that she was shaking with cold.

'I'll be all right. You carry on,' she said, but I could see in her eyes that we had to get back to shelter quickly. Trout continued to gulp down the duns as we turned and started a thirty-minute walk back to the car.

***

A few kilometres upstream, near where East Dome, the high point of the Mataura Range, and the Garvie Mountains squeeze the valley tight to the river, I found an area where the Mataura had, during the recent flood, cut off a large loop and removed a backwater that had been there for the forty years I had fished the gorge. The new channel took the river straight into a high bank of blue-grey clay which it hit with such energy that a plume of blue mist discoloured the river as it headed downstream. Above the clay bank the river was clear.

I passed through this part of the gorge for the first time in the mid-1970s. That journey was downstream, in a Canadian canoe, with my brother-in-law Geoff. It was a craft I had little experience with, and we tipped out before we had travelled a hundred metres, but we eventually found a way to stay upright. However, in the loop now cut off by the changed river course, we ended up pushed sideways against a rock wall with the river threatening to roll us into the roiling depths. On that trip we camped in the middle of the gorge. When we stood by the river contemplating breakfast that first morning I foolishly said, 'If you light a fire, I'll catch a trout for breakfast.' It would have been a reckless promise at any time, but was particularly so that morning because I had only been back in the south for a few months and my skills with a fly rod left much to be desired. Remarkably, the first trout I saw was blessed with even less wit than me, and even though my first cast landed well to one side it sidled over, took my nymph and was soon in the net. Geoff watched me from the fire with a broad smile behind his large red beard.

'Good on ya,' he said when I ambled back, trout flailing in the net, as though he never doubted that I would catch one.

***

The upstream breeze had died, the morning cloud burnt off, and I followed the river west under a pale blue sky. The beech-clad flanks of East Dome reached close to the water, near where a couple of creeks joined the Mataura over fans of chunky rock. This large material helps form the stable home for the mayfly and caddis that make this part of the river so productive. The river here is easily waded at the bottom end of the pools, before the river begins to accelerate into the ripples that appear every few hundred metres. The bush, surrounding mountains, and the speed and bounce of the river in the gorge lend a backcountry feel to the area. The sounds of bellbirds and tūī echoed across the valley, and a pīwakawaka attempted to land on my extended walking stick when I slowed to admire it.

For a few moments I knelt beside the rutted farm track to look at a koura stranded in a little pool a couple of metres above the river. When I looked up I saw a kārearea perched on a gate post watching me. Once, these raptors would have ranged widely across Southland, but much of their habitat has been destroyed and they are a rare sight now. Over the years my angling friends have seen what appears to have been a single family or group of kārearea living in the gorge. Once, JD and I watched what looked to be an adult bird drop a mouse which was grabbed by the talons of a juvenile bird flying below, as though it was being taught a lesson. In the spring they have, once in a while, buzzed me at high speed, warning me off with a screech, but this bird sat on the post and watched me approach. When I was about ten paces away it turned its head side-on to me, profiling its imperious hooked beak, and I stopped under the gaze of its fearless eye. It watched me for a minute or so until it heard an aircraft that approached from the east. It swivelled its gaze towards the sound and followed the plane until it disappeared over the ridges in the west. I edged closer, wishing that my camera was in my hand and not zipped into the top compartment of my pack. The bird crouched in readiness to fly, but instead of launching itself towards the bush it dropped to the ground just a rod-length away. For a few moments it bobbed its head while it fixed me in its gaze, then lifted back to the top of the post. Eventually it swooped towards me, passing so close that I flung my head away like a batsman dodging a bouncer. It was the closest I had ever been to a kārearea and it left my heart thudding. Twenty years earlier I would have called the bird a falcon without giving a thought to differentiating it from falcons in other countries. Calling it a New Zealand falcon sounds too prosaic for my liking, so when I see them now the word that comes to me is 'kārearea'.

Once through the gate I sat in the sun, watching the river as it sped over a drop-off into a deep pool beside a rock the size of a small house. While I ate a handful of nuts I heard the kārearea's screech and turned to see it flying low over my seat on the riverbank and landing on the track, about twenty metres ahead. It held what looked like a mouse under one of its talons. While it tore the little animal apart with its beak, I unzipped my pack and grabbed my camera. I edged towards it, taking photos as I went because getting much closer felt unlikely. When it finished eating it flew towards me, landing on a dead branch just six or seven paces away; close enough for me see it preen the bloodied rust-brown feathers around its beak. The feathers on its cape were fine and dark, like high-cocoa chocolate. It cleaned itself with beak and talons for around five minutes while I stood as still as I could, watching it in awe. Eventually it flew off in a blur of feathers, swooping low over the Mataura before disappearing into the forest.

On the ground where the kārearea had consumed her prey I found a few spots of blood and a couple of small yellow feathers, indicating she had devoured a bird, and not a mouse as I first thought. Just a year earlier I had read J. A. Baker's *The Peregrine*, a beautifully told story of that raptor in which the writer revealed a personal obsession with peregrines that went close to madness. He described how, when he crouched over the remnants of the peregrine's kill, for a moment at least he felt that he too had become a raptor. I didn't feel that as I knelt over the remains of the yellow-head, but I was so moved by being close to the wildness of the falcon that I felt a tear or two on my cheeks. The next day was to be my sixty-eighth birthday, and I figured that the close encounter with the kārearea was a good omen.

By late afternoon I reached the twenty-kilometre mark on my

topographical map. While my legs were starting to feel heavy, hours of daylight remained and the ground ahead was open and easy, so I pushed on. While cutting off a couple of horseshoe bends where the valley twists north I came across an angler fishing up the far bank — the first person I had encountered on the river that day. We waved and I moved on along the tussock-covered terrace below Myrtle Hut. I slept in the hut once years ago, and, while it was tempting to do it again, I hadn't asked for permission, so decided against stopping.

The river flows towards the terrace below the hut with almost no deviation for close to three kilometres along a valley floor, broad in the north and tighter at the Myrtle Hut end. The Garvie Mountains reach towards the eastern side of the river in a series of gently sloping terraces, while a steep-sided ridge runs parallel to the river in the west. The broad flats ahead had recently been worked with plough and disc, and the new grass looked emerald green against the backdrop of dark bush and tussock.

Forty-five minutes later I found a spot to camp beside the river, near the low saddle between the Mataura and Dome Creek. I lay back in the grass, eased off my new boots, and decided I needed coffee before erecting my tent. Two fine trout hung in the current just a pace or two away from my seat on a log. Once in a while their snouts sliced through the surface as they sucked mayfly duns into their creamy mouths. They looked easy targets, but without a fly rod all I could do was sip my coffee and admire the awful beauty of their performance. While they took many flies, most were left to drift briefly downstream before lifting unmolested into the evening air. I tried to recall where I had read someone describe the life cycle of the mayfly, culminating as it does in the transformation from a life spent mostly under water to a brief but miraculous period when they unfold diaphanous wings that carry them to the land, where they settle for a day or two on stream-side trees and grasses. For their final act they exchange their outer skin for another, even more delicate than the first, before returning to the air above the river. I've often watched them, backlit by evening light, dancing in a mating ritual above the smooth glides, before the females caress the water with their tails to dislodge the eggs that complete the circle of their lives. The author said it was 'as extraordinary as the migration of the wildebeest'.

Two small aircraft droned up the valley at low level, as though looking for a place to land. They belonged to a couple of friends — Terry in his bright-yellow Carbon Cub, and Dave in his blue Rans. They flew past me before turning back and settling into a low-speed approach towards a paddock near my camping spot. I hoped they had flown in a shot or two of vodka to share but they hadn't, and soon were headed down the gorge towards Balfour, leaving me to cook my freeze-dried meal in the rapidly cooling air. I remained hungry even after consuming a packet of risotto that was supposed to feed two, so I followed it with custard and dried apricots.

Back at the log, I watched the river trace a silver scar through the darkening land. The moon climbed into a pale sky, while a pink light grazed the ridges of the Garvies. The solitude was, I thought, the perfect lead-in to my birthday, just a few hours away. The light upstream breeze carried a hint of wood smoke, a comforting smell that reminds me of only the best of times. I guessed the smoke came from a fire lit by the angler I had seen earlier. The land was silent, apart from the murmur of the river and the hoot of a ruru from the edge of the bush.

I was moved by the place, as I have been almost every time I've ventured into this gorge. A line from Adam Haslett's sombre novel *Imagine Me Gone* came to me. That's it, I thought: 'It's the landscape of my happiness.' I find it impossible to be in these big, solitary landscapes without reflecting on what this life is about and my position on the rapidly advancing conveyor belt of our existence. It's in these places I can contemplate the course of my life without it turning into a sweaty dread.

BIRTHDAY

At three I woke in the cold, unzipped the tent, and poked my head into the night. Galaxies were piled above; the moon looked blue with cold. While I waited on sleep I listened to Leonard Cohen on earplugs from my phone: his latest album, *You Want it Darker*, pensive, sad, but oddly comforting to me that night I turned sixty-eight.

By 4.50 a.m. I was awake again, feeling too cold and excited about the day ahead to go back to sleep. Long johns, wool socks, a merino undershirt and a tramping jersey weren't enough to overcome the lack of insulation in my much-used sleeping bag. I had thought about buying a flash new one for the trip but wrongly assumed that it wouldn't be needed on this mid-summer walk. With my knees curled up to my chest for warmth I contemplated this day of my birth while I waited for the light to fill the valley. I was only two years from the biblical allocation of three score and ten, and it felt improbable to have reached this stage of my life. When I was a teenager I was so surrounded by death that I convinced myself my chances of making it to old age were slim — yet here I was, in this remarkable time, midway between the explosive formation of the planet and its likely frozen end. It wasn't apprehension or fear that I felt, more an increasing sense of wonder at my existence. I thought again about the kārearea and the sense of connection I felt with it as I looked into its indifferent eyes. It was the wildness of it that captivated me then, and had me thinking about it again.

The previous evening I had fallen asleep while reading *The Moth Snowstorm* by Michael McCarthy. In it he described how, when he was a skinny kid in short pants, butterflies entered his soul. His experience felt like a mirror of my early entrancement with trout and the places they inhabit. It felt a fitting coincidence that I began reading his book after spending an evening sitting beside the Mataura, watching a couple of large trout set aside their innate caution and begin rising to duns, sending rings of disturbance across the darkening surface of the river. McCarthy also described the fear he felt when close to wild animals, but mixed in with the fear of being near, say, an African buffalo was a feeling of living more intensely. He thinks that these feelings are lodged deep inside us, and emerge to surprise. It was a natural thing, he said, because 'we have worked in neon-lit offices for a mere four or five generations, but were farmers before that for five hundred generations, and hunter gatherers for perhaps fifty thousand or more before that'. This might explain the way I felt when I looked into the eyes of the kārearea, or what I feel when I look into the eyes of a trout, permit or ancient-looking tarpon. It taps into something that goes all the way back to my hunter-gatherer forebears perhaps, and can't be done away with.

The colour of the day returned slowly. It started as grey, cold as a cadaver, and moved slowly over the next hour until my tent glowed. I listened to the river while I waited on warmth. In the past I've used words like 'murmur' and 'gurgle' to describe the sound of moving water. I closed my eyes and concentrated on the sound to try to get a fix on it. Apart from a couple of gulls screeching and the call of a ruru, the river was all I could hear. Slowly a picture of the sound formed. It sounded like wind blowing through leafy trees, though it wasn't the movement of air that I was hearing — it was like the sound of the leaves moving and colliding with each other. It rose and fell as though the tone of the river changed in tune with a hidden pulse.

With the sunlight halfway down the western flanks of the gorge, I unzipped the tent; dressed awkwardly in the tight space; and stepped out to find the tent fly, pack and boots covered with a rime of frost in what was supposed to be summer. The sky was blue, and the air still.

I warmed my hands with a cup of coffee while sitting on a log beside the flow. A ghost of fog hung over the river, as though it was as hot as the coffee. From the high ridges above me I heard dogs barking and then the voices of men echoing in the hills. Single white dots became moving threads across the tussock-covered faces, and before long masses of sheep rolled across the slopes like a creamy cloud gone to ground, pushed along by dogs and musterers.

When the sunlight finally made its way over the valley floor to my camp, I splashed my face with river water, packed my gear and started walking north, buoyed to be in this country and with the thought that Sue would later meet me in Athol to help celebrate my birthday.

The morning started with a bash through a tangle of gorse along the riparian strip before I crossed the achingly cold flow and headed upstream over sheep-manicured paddocks on the broadening valley floor. After an hour I came across a fly angler working carefully up a high bank. I held back and watched him. He threw a series of tight-looped casts, each time landing the dry fly in a pocket of slack water, close to an overhang of grass. While no trout rose to the fly, I could see he was skilled from the tightness of the loops of line that unfurled from his rod to the delicacy of the presentation of the fly. When he stepped back from the river I waved and walked up for a chat. He was from Auckland — Mark was his name — and like me he had roots in the south. He started life in Southland, went to Auckland by way of Dunedin, and spent some time working overseas. He looked a corporate type and had fine-looking gear, with a Go-Pro strapped to his cap to catch the action. 'I come here once or twice a year,' he said. 'This northern part of the gorge is my favourite place anywhere. Even if I'm not catching fish I feel at home. There's a beauty that keeps pulling me back.'

I stayed away from the bank for a while to avoid sending the trout scurrying from their feeding lanes into the bottom of the deep bouldery pools where they might skulk for hours. The river hugged the steep beech-covered flanks to the west: where it curved towards me in a series of ripples and runs, fragments of sunlight danced from the broken surface. There is a perfection to the river as it pushes through this section of the gorge. The chunky stones and rocks on the bed of the river are relatively stable, making it a brilliant place for mayflies and caddis. On the river's true right, close in to the steep land that climbs away to the west, a few deep holes have formed beside the food-rich ripples. It's about as good as rivers get, but is challenged now by increased pressure from guides — and others like me who simply love the place and have the time on our hands to be there.

As I walked on I thought about a friend who landed a trout in this area while under arrest. He thinks he's likely to be the only person in New Zealand to have done it. Back then he was dobbed in by a couple of anglers who had walked into the gorge early. They saw a bag of fertiliser sitting outside his tent and, after deciding that the operation wasn't part of the farm's activities, informed the police who arrested my friend for growing marijuana. While walking out to the road with a couple of policemen for company, my friend spotted a trout rising steadily. 'Do you mind if I have a cast, officer?' he asked, and while the police watched from the bank he waded in, unfurled a beautiful cast that placed the fly inches above the snout of the big trout — which took it. While the police might have been impressed by his magical fishing, they didn't think that it was an act of sufficient grace to let him off, so he carried on to the road with the trout swinging from his belt.

***

Where my route beside the river twisted sharply east, close to the start of the Nokomai Station farm track, I came across an angler standing on a high bank, watching two large trout gliding close to the surface of a deep pool. He was from Canberra, and he said he came to fish in this part of the world regularly. I pushed on past Paddy's Milestone, a conical oddity, probably sliced away from the Garvies thousands of years earlier by the much larger river that once thundered through this gorge.

Late morning, with a shimmer of heat over the land, I lay back in the summer grass and listened to an unnamed spring creek flow beside me. I checked it on my map. It started life in a wetland a kilometre or so away. I knelt beside the creek to wash the cold water over my face and head, before taking some deep gulps. With the map opened to check on the distance I had travelled that morning, I was struck by the hundreds of unnamed creeks marked on it like blue veins, flowing out of the high country before gathering in the bush-clad valleys on their way to the Mataura. Lying back looking at puffy summer clouds drifting in from the west I thought about the first time I fished this part of the gorge. It was in November, in the late 1970s. JD and I fished together in a spring storm that blew sleety showers in from the south. That day the river was cold, and coloured a milky blue by snowmelt. We had no fancy waders back then — I wore a pair of old suit pants worn too thin and shiny in the backside for work, and JD wore jeans. It was gloriously easy fishing, with duns popping off the ripples that were stacked with trout feeding without guile. Around 2 p.m. JD said he was too cold to continue, and while I was driven to catch every trout around when I was thirty I didn't have it in me to push on, so with fish still feeding hard on the hatching duns we retreated to the shelter of JD's car and shivered our way out of the gorge, waiting on the pathetic heater in his Datsun to throw us some warmth.

***

After crossing the Nokomai Stream I walked on the gravel road as it followed the river west. Nokomai Station has a number of well-sign-posted access points through this section of river — well spaced, with clearly spelt-out rights and obligations for those wishing to cross private property. The Station has created an area where travellers are able to camp overnight beside the river free of charge, though they have stopped anglers and others driving down into the gorge on farm tracks. On balance, it felt like a realistic response to the burgeoning increase in angling that risks over-running the upper river.

About a kilometre upstream of the first bridge above the gorge I stopped to talk with an Irish-Australian angler who was reading by the roadside. Fergus, an engineer from Brisbane, had damaged his knee in a fall while fishing, and was having a day off. I was tired after a day and half of solid walking so was happy to spend twenty minutes in the shade chatting about the river and my walk. His angling companion, Trevor, joined us as I was about to move on. I recognised his name from a Facebook post where he was shown with a fine Cape York permit. We chuckled at the smallness of the angling world. His guide on the day he landed his permit was Jason Owens, the guide I was with when I landed my best-ever Cape York permit.

Near a cluster of fishing cottages I saw the first female angler I had encountered on the trip. We walked towards each other for about fifty metres before we passed. Something about her look — best boots and waders, even though the day was warm — and the way she dressed suggested that she wasn't from New Zealand. I said hello as we passed but she wasn't prepared to make eye contact, and with the hint of a smile she moved on. Her muted response felt unfriendly at first, but it reminded me that while it is commonplace for New Zealanders to speak to total strangers in those circumstances, this isn't necessarily true in many Western countries.

Half an hour later I found Rick's car on a bluff overlooking the river. He wasn't there, so I lay in the grass and snacked on nuts while I waited. Rick eventually arrived and offered to take my pack on to Athol. I left him fishing while I moved upstream around the southern toe of Slate Range, stopping for a moment to watch two trout doing slow circuits of a willow-shaded backwater, sipping willow grubs as they went.

***

Soon after Dad returned from World War II he and my grandfather worked in a Post and Telegraph gang in this area, installing telegraph poles and lines. Mum has a photograph of a thinner version of Dad than I remember, bare-topped, wearing old army shorts, and perched on a rock beside the river. Mum said the two men stayed in the Parawa Hotel. The hotel, built in 1867 to service travellers heading to and from the Otago goldfields and mines in the area, now sits derelict on the junction of the road down Nokomai Gorge and the Queenstown–Five Rivers Highway, passed daily by a stream of camper vans and tourist buses.

Beside a deep pool formed where the river glides past a truncated spur I stripped off and floated in the current, imagining that Dad might have swum in the same pool seventy years earlier — as he did in a photograph Mum has of him taken in the late 1940s, up to his neck in the river.

This stretch of the Mataura from Parawa to Garston was mostly new to me. Despite our miserable summer not encouraging a plentiful fall of willow grubs, as I walked through this heavily willowed section a few solid trout sipped the tiny grubs from the slick surface. The emergence of willow grubs (larvae of the willow sawfly) signals the start of the most demanding months of my angling year. In what looks like a misstep in the evolutionary process, the willow grubs have been paired up with trees that often grow beside water, meaning most of the grubs fall into streams where they meet an end nourishing trout or drifting into oblivion. It's remarkable to me that while almost every willow leaf hosts a larva, and the life cycle of the grub is short, I've never seen the wasp-like adults laying their eggs. The life cycle of the sawfly appears to occupy an absurdly narrow niche that impacts on the willows, which thrive despite the predation; the trout, for whom they are a rich source of food; and fly fishers, who expose themselves to the potential for humiliation as they attempt to deceive trout into taking their imitation ahead of the multitude of grubs. Nothing else appears to have a stake in a game that few know is even being played. On warm breezy days during summer, most of the few trout that I keep these days have had their stomachs packed tight with grubs. When I've tried to count them I can usually get to a hundred or so before I give up, thinking that there must be three or four hundred in the stomach. By my rough calculation, each trout in the willowed sections of the Mataura probably consumes between ten and fifteen thousand grubs a season.

***

The valley continued to broaden as I headed towards Athol with the river flowing through avenues of willows. Finer gravels filled the riverbed as I got closer to the confluence with Eyre Creek. This stream drains the precipitous catchment between Eyre Peak in the north and Jane Peak to the south, and while its normal flow is barely a cumec, during heavy rain in the mountains it hurtles down the tight valley, carrying with it fine gravels swept off a couple of unstable faces. A few months earlier Randy Rummel and I took my Land Rover up Eyre Creek as far as Shepherd Creek hut and walked beyond there towards Dog Box bivouac. We found few trout but that failure didn't matter, because we were enthralled by the mountains that loomed over us, and the emerald water bouncing down the valley. The night we spent there we cooked beans and seared a couple of steaks in a heavy skillet over the last glow of embers from our fire, and sat under a mantle of stars with a single-malt whisky talking about the trajectory of our lives. We've been friends for thirty years, but still find it easier to talk about the things that really matter to us away from it all, in these beautiful valleys, with just the sound of the fire crackling and the stream in the background. In earlier years I might have found the lack of trout a disappointment but we left this one thinking it was perhaps the high point of Randy's visit from the States. In a way, it took my desire to possess trout — to trap the beauty of them in my hands — to lure me into these places, but at this time in my life I've held enough of them to be almost released from their thrall, freeing me to enjoy the places they take me. Most of the time.

***

After checking my map I thought there was a chance I would be late for my rendezvous with Rick at Riverview bridge, so I left the river and headed for Paddys Alley Road where I expected to make up time. I climbed under the first fence and made for the road, but soon found my way blocked by a series of three-wire electric fences. After some searching, I managed to slide under the bottom wire of the fence where it crossed a culvert and, watched by hundreds of cows, waded up a well-fenced creek that snaked towards the road. Leaving the creek required another Houdini-like effort, as did finally getting to the road where I crawled up a ditch and passed close enough to a wire to allow an arc of electricity to jolt me through my sodden, mud-caked, trousers. Worn out, and thinking I was going to be late for Rick, I headed north on the gravel road where I was confronted with a couple of signs stating there was no access to the river through the property I had just left.

Near the bridge the river curved back towards the road, and for a time the gap between the two was less than twenty metres — a space normally occupied by the Queen's Chain, which allows anglers and others to access the river. However, the farmer had fixed an impenetrable five-strand electric fence so close to the edge of the road that there wasn't even a grassy verge to walk on, let alone access to the river. By the time I saw Rick standing on the bridge I was tired and fuming at the injustice of it all. It was the first instance I found on the river where the fencing appeared to have more to do with denying access than for any legitimate farming need.

'You know, last year I risked falling into the river in flood to help save one of their ewes,' I said to Rick. 'She was tangled in barbed wire, down a steep bank and half-submerged. Just upstream of the bridge. Evans reckoned I would've been a goner if I'd slipped, but having seen her pleading eyes I couldn't walk away. Would've been a slow cold death. I'm feeling pissed off now that I did something to help the owner of this place though.'

I had a beer with Rick before he left for Wanaka, and when Sue arrived we ate fish and chips in the courtyard of the Brown Trout Cafe and had a drink to celebrate my birthday. A long walk through a landscape that I love, a simple meal and a quiet evening spent close to the river with Sue was as much as I could have hoped for.

Our hut in the campground was separated from the river by a paddock. In the warm evening we walked Izzy and Knut past the mostly young tourists, tanned and lean, the smell of boiling noodles drifting from portable stoves outside tents and vans while T-shirts, knickers and underpants hung from makeshift lines. A young Frenchwoman with startlingly dark brown eyes spoke to us in the fading light and patted the dogs who, for a moment, looked up at her before they turned back to the alpacas which had followed us along the fence line.

On the edge of sleep we were startled by a flood of light into our room as a car crunched to a halt outside. Bugger, I thought, hoping this late arrival wouldn't wake the dogs settled in Sue's car. Moments after the sliding door on the unit beside us clunked shut, our neighbour started coughing, the sound carrying to us as though the wall between us was made of paper. While we whispered, the cough raged on, deep, phlegmy and insistent. I sniffed suspiciously at my pillow and wondered what similar indignities it had been exposed to before weariness sent me to sleep.

Dave and JD, back in the 80s.

The author and Uncle Ernie. My fishing mate, in the 70s.

Start of the walk. Where the Mataura meets the ocean.

PHOTO CREDIT: DOUGAL RILLSTONE

Saying goodbye to Sue at the start of the walk.

PHOTO CREDIT: SUE LARKINS

Camp beside the lower Mataura.
PHOTO CREDIT: DOUGAL RILLSTONE

Whitebaiter's accommodation on the estuary.
PHOTO CREDIT: DOUGAL RILLSTONE

A day's walk in from the coast.

Looking towards the falls, the meat works and paper mill.

Mataura passing through seams of rock, above Gore.
PHOTO CREDIT: DOUGAL RILLSTONE

Karearea in the Nokomai Gorge.
PHOTO CREDIT: DOUGAL RILLSTONE

Near the end of the walk, looking towards the source in the Eyre Mountains.
PHOTO CREDIT: DOUGAL RILLSTONE

Dougal, close to the source.
PHOTO CREDIT: DOUGAL RILLSTONE

Dougal on point in the Waimea.
PHOTO CREDIT: SUE LARKINS

Kevin Ireland casting at trout rising in the foam line.
PHOTO CREDIT: DOUGAL RILLSTONE

Dave, ebullient, on the Waimea.

JD, on the Mataura.

Late light on the Mataura upstream of Athol.

The mayfly hatch can look like a blizzard.

Late in the season, near Fairlight.

PHOTO CREDIT: ANDREW HARDING

They keep us coming back.

Trout often hang where casting is a challenge.

The Waikaia Valley.

Cattle continue to break down banks, and pollute the river.

Perfection.

ATHOL TO FAIRLIGHT

After waking, I lay tucked in beside Sue, feeling her warmth, while I took a moment to delete a pile of emails that had caught up with me after two days without internet coverage. On a final scan of the messages headed for the bin I spotted an opening line in one that caught my attention. Under a name I didn't recognise I saw the words, 'We liked your story and would . . .' I nudged Sue awake. 'I can't believe it. I think I've received a reply from *Gray's* [*Sporting Journal* in Augusta, Georgia]. I think they like my bloody story.'

'Have you looked at it? Open it,' said Sue.

'I'm not opening it till the walk's finished. The fact they've replied is enough. I can't face the message right now. I'm happy to just bask in the fact they like it.'

I felt as though I was fifteen again, standing at our letter box in Wentworth Street, holding the envelope containing my School Certificate results, looking back at Mum watching me from the kitchen window, her eyes urging me to open it, but knowing that I couldn't — not right then.

'Don't be stupid,' said Sue.

'I'm not, and don't you dare,' I said as I headed to the shower block. Sue was feeding the dogs when I returned. Back in the room I reread the heading details of the email, and when I noticed the blue dot indicating that the email was unread had disappeared I looked towards Sue who flashed back an enigmatic look. She didn't look sad, so I opened the message. 'Fuck me! They not only like it, but they want to publish it!' I said as I bounced out of the room.

'Well done you,' said Sue.

'Dangerous thing to do, opening other people's emails,' I said, but she just laughed.

My parting from Sue wasn't as painful as when she dropped me off at the start of the walk. I was buoyed by the news from *Gray's*, and by the thought that the birthplace of the river in the Eyre Mountains was tantalisingly close.

I left Athol on the bike trail which followed the course of the railway line that ran through the valley from 1878 until it was closed in 1979. For the second day running I started with the sound of sheep being mustered — dogs barking, men yelling and whistling on the slopes of Slate Range. Sheep accumulated as if by magic from the tussock-covered slopes. The wind blew hard and warm out of the north-west. It had been almost a month since I started the walk and I could see the change in the angle of the sun. Shadows were thrown further, and even though autumn was a few weeks away the light already carried the sharpness of seasonal change.

The Mataura, a pale shade of turquoise, ran under the new bridge built to carry the cyclists now using the track. In mid-current a large trout held position behind a boulder, the flick of its tail and subtle changes in the angle of its pectoral fins enough to hold it in place. Another two fish rode the currents on the edge of the eroded holes above the bridge piles. These flighty creatures usually dive for cover when a person enters their sight, but near bridges they sometimes act as though they've worked out that passing humans aren't a threat.

Upstream of the bridge the banks on the eastern side are manicured by sheep, giving the river the look of an English spring creek rather than a New Zealand freestone river. I headed upstream on the true left bank, keeping away from the rougher country on the western side where the river pushes against the hills. The bed of the Mataura in this area is relatively stable, with a perfect mix of fist-sized stones and gravel. In the shallow ripples, mayfly nymphs darted from the tops of the stones at my approach, as though I was a threat to them. Almost every time I am near a stream I pick up stones, because they are one of the best indicators of the health of the water. This day the top side of the stones were coated with a light film of algae, making them slippery to touch. Their undersides teemed with caddis larvae glued to the surface and mayfly nymphs in various stages of maturity.

I first passed through this area back in the 1950s on a trip to Queenstown. We travelled from Gore to Kingston on the train, and then on to Queenstown on the T.S.S. *Earnslaw*. I felt excited to be travelling to such a far-off place. The landscape I saw from the train between Nokomai and Fairlight probably looked much as it does today because farming in that part of the valley hasn't changed much but the road, which sixty years ago when I first saw it carried few cars and buses, is now a busy tourist highway.

A couple of paddocks east of my track beside the river a stream of cars, buses and campervans rumbled past, hurrying to the next must-see place. On the few occasions I fish this part of the river and amble back to my vehicle along the roadside towards the end of the day, wearing waders and holding my fly rod, I often catch glimpses of faces staring at me from the oncoming traffic as though I'm an apparition.

It isn't just the road that has become busy. The upper Mataura, once protected from overuse by poor roads and distance, and consequently fished by few, is now inundated with fly fishers, many of whom arrive at the international airport an hour up the road. (When I first saw the airfield, it was nothing more than a dry-looking paddock, with grass strips used by a couple of Dominies, Tiger Moths and the odd Cessna.) From December until the last week of the season in April, they compete to get to the access points — generously offered by the local farming families — as early as possible, hoping to find a stretch of river to themselves. I find it hard to blame them because the fishery remains world-class, and by the standards of the places many of them come from it is uncrowded. However, for those of us who fished here before the influx of tourist anglers, the experience has been diminished, mostly because the solitude — the chance to fish for a day without running into others — has largely gone. It looks to me like a modern-day playing out of the 'tragedy of the commons', where there isn't an incentive for any one angler or guide to limit their use of the river in the interests of others. Those of us who knew the river before the surge in tourist anglers have mostly moved on to less-crowded water, or seek out the short period between the river becoming fishable in the spring and the arrival of these mostly foreign fishers.

***

In one of those periods of solitude a couple of years before my walk up the river, I fished the area with JD late in October. That day the river ran full and was coloured by a haze of snowmelt. Fresh snow contoured low around the hills and cold showers rolled in from the south. Perhaps because it looked to be a day without promise, ours was the only car parked at the bridge.

'It'll be good in an hour or two when the sun warms the water. Reckon there'll be a hatch,' I said, trying to sound positive.

'Everything else is out. Can't think of another option,' said JD, sounding more resigned than optimistic.

We had gone only a couple of hundred metres when the milky-green water began to erode my confidence. I checked my fly-box for a woolly bugger or feathered lure, thinking that fishing down and across, something I do just once every decade or so, might tempt a trout from the depths. Finding none in my vest, I headed back to the car to find my lures, relegated through lack of use to the bottom of my tackle bag. I swung a woolly bugger down and across some deep runs and under willows on the far bank, but the technique felt alien. Years earlier I had thought fishing this way was something I could get into but I couldn't find any rhythm in what I was doing, and the lure swung unconvincingly through the current. It's not a form of fishing that brings me any pleasure, so I gave up after a couple of runs, tied on two small nymphs, and walked upstream, exploring the water while looking for feeding trout.

The trout remained hidden until mid-afternoon. Then, through gaps in the willow, we began to see them, deep down, swaying in the current, once in a while showing the white flash from the inside of their mouths as they took nymphs. Moving upstream, crouching close to the vegetation for cover, I failed to find a place where I could get a cast at them. Eventually, in some shallow bouncy water above a ripple, I saw rings extending away from the centre of a rise — for me, the most magical sight in trout fishing. Taking on the pose of a heron working the shallows, I searched for the fish which showed first as an ephemeral shadow on the stream bed. My eyes aren't what they were, but sixty years of looking into water for trout allowed my brain to process these fragments of shadow and reflected light into the solidity of a trout. On my first cast the fish leaned in the direction of the passing nymphs but didn't take. Moments later it took a fly from the surface film. Distracting ripples at the edge of my vision added to the challenge of tying on a size 16 snowshoe-hare emerger. The fish ignored the first couple of casts which were slightly wide of the mark, before rising with certainty to take the fly the first time it tracked over its nose. I landed it quickly and moved on.

A tangle of willows and gorse slowed my progress and I was

forced to lower myself into the current and use willow roots and long grass on the bank to haul myself upstream. I stumbled forward in the waist-deep current that threatened to loosen my tenuous hold on the bottom. The water looked black and hard, as though surfaced with a metallic sheen, in the shadow of the trees and the high bank.

Seams of rock lay close to the surface above me, curving the water over and around their polished surfaces. When I see water doing this, I'm reminded of a poem by Vincent O'Sullivan (from his 2011 collection *The movie may be slightly different*), a print of which hangs from a wall at home in Dunedin. It begins:

> If you like, in this light,
> The river clips against three rocks
> As though three brides are rising
> From the current.
> They set
> Out in different directions,
> The river trails behind them,
> The long aisle of each bride.

The nose of a trout broke the surface a metre above the closest rock seam as it intercepted a dark mayfly dun from the squadron of duns that pirouetted towards me. When the trout had settled back into its feeding position, I landed my imitation dun on the seam of current that carried the hatching mayflies into the path of the trout. The trout lifted towards my fly, but in that moment I saw tiny contrails of disturbed water trail behind it, and the big fish turned away, sensing as I did that something was amiss. Numerous roll casts and a couple of flies lost to the edge of the rock seam later, I landed the dun close enough to the trout, with just enough crumple in the leader to allow it to drift, drag-free, and the trout took it with indifference.

Over the next fifty metres, close in to the bank, and under a roof of willows which made conventional casting impossible, I hooked another six fish, most around four pounds. One took me into the backing, and because I wasn't able to follow it downstream it broke free. The trout I netted were heavy-shouldered, and hard as a weightlifter's biceps. This intimate, visual, tough, dry-fly-fishing is one of the reasons I am drawn back to the river season after season. My friends and I cherish those few days we have on this part of the river, when it is devoid of others and the fishing is as brilliant as it was in the best of our memories.

***

I continued upstream watching the buffeting wind and fragments of sun play on the long dry grasses, which rippled and swayed like a giant sculpture. Red-clover flowers had started to brown, and in the paddock I lay beside for my morning break, just the woolly backs of the sheep were visible above the sea of pink flowering thistle heads, whose downy seeds were unleashed to the boisterous sky. Closer to the river the willow leaves, vibrant green in spring and summer, had turned a dull olive. Ahead, wind-sculpted lenticular clouds held station in the crystal light, high above the southern end of the Hector Mountains.

Further along the old rail track I sheltered from the wind in the lee of a stunted apple tree. Its small apples and scrawny visage spoke of the long chilling winters experienced in the valley, and the hot dry summers that often followed.

I left the rail trail above the disused Nokomai siding and followed the eastern bank of the Mataura to Garston. The river appeared to shrink as I moved north. Remarkably, I saw no anglers on this section of the upper river. The big trout I found were easily spooked, but when I approached them carefully, using long grass and willows to hide my profile, I managed to get within a couple of rod-lengths. Without the urgency I feel when I'm carrying a rod, I took the time to watch them feed.

They operated in the water with the same grace that I saw in the tiny dark swallows and chaffinches that flew above the stream, plucking at the few mayflies that climbed like tiny grey helicopters from the surface.

At Garston I left the river at the bridge and walked into the settlement. Just one of the three hotels that were there in its best days remains, but it has a school on a terrace above the river, a picturesque Presbyterian church, and a shop selling antique furniture from a building once used to stable passing horses. Garston is reputed to be further from the ocean than any other place in New Zealand, although I know of one other town making that claim.

There is a positive side to the number of tourists travelling on this road: good coffee has arrived. I bought a flat white and salmon bagel from the Coffee Bomb, which operates from an Airstream caravan, sleek and shiny under the noon sun. On a nearby seat I took off my boots; wrung the water from my socks and dried my feet, wrinkled as though I had spent too long in a bath; and ate the bagel which was as good as any I have tasted.

Upstream of the Garston bridge I watched a fly fisher casting at a rising trout, and when the fish eventually slid away into the shadows I walked up and spoke to him. He appeared about my age, was fit-looking with sun creases etched into his face and neck, and spoke with a strong Scottish accent. We talked of the river which he knew as a regular visitor and had grown to cherish.

A few bends further on I stopped to watch a young Japanese angler casting to a trout that rose close to a dipping curtain of willows. Her fly eventually hooked a branch and while she was in the process of shaking it free she saw me standing downstream. While careful to avoid catching my eye, she smiled towards the water before going on to retrieve her fly. Around the next curve I saw a Japanese man, who I assumed was her partner, crouched low on a gravel beach with two trout that looked about five pounds each, feeding a short cast upstream. Another fish patrolled the edge of a drop-off a few metres above the first two. While he looked towards the trout, he held a phone to his ear and spoke with the intensity of someone participating in a breakfast meeting in Tokyo, not that I was able to decipher a thing he said. It's possible, I suppose, that he had been driven to distraction by the cussedness of the fish and had decided to call someone for advice on how to catch them — but I doubt it. I wanted to explain to him I was about to move upstream, and wasn't fishing so wouldn't disturb his day, but even though I stood just ten paces from him he didn't acknowledge me.

My path upstream followed the river as it angled out of the north-west, away from the striated face climbing steeply above the true left bank. This is where the Bright Water spring enters the Mataura. The Bright Water issues from the ground close to the slopes above Fairlight Station, and where it enters the river makes up close to a third of its normal flow: a cool, constant gift to the Mataura. It holds some extraordinary trout that spend much of their time hidden under banks and among the rich plant life that thrives in the clear water, but most days, around the middle of the afternoon, they come out to feed on hatching mayflies.

Just a few kilometres upstream of the confluence, potential danger exists for both the Bright Water and the Mataura. Some of the land on the thin soil over the terminal moraine south of Lake Wakatipu has been recently irrigated with water taken from bores, and for the first time in the sixty years or so I have known the area, intensive agriculture appears to be on the way. There is plenty of evidence to show what the likely outcome of this will be: excessive nutrient enrichment of the creeks that flow into the Mataura, and the inevitable degradation of water quality in this high part of the catchment. I'm saddened by the short-sightedness of it.

A pair of angler's trousers, enigmatically hanging from a car window at the end of Bright Water Road, flapped in the breeze as I walked past. Upstream of the car I saw bootprints in the fine gravel, sharp-edged and unworn by wind or rain, suggesting that the possible owner of the trousers wasn't far ahead.

The river, already reduced in size above the Bright Water, appeared to shrink further as though some of the flow was being lost, through the fine gravels, to the water table below. It now bore little resemblance to the river I started my walk bedside as it tipped into the Southern Ocean a couple of hundred kilometres to the south. Here, ever closer to its source, it tumbled and bounced past, throwing off flashes of light as though its bed was made up of fist-sized diamonds.

Over the next kilometre the river made a curving run across open ground. I guessed the angler ahead of me had put the trout down because I saw just one in that mostly treeless stretch, but my assumption was quickly proved wrong. Soon after I followed the river into an avenue of willows I found trout feeding on willow grubs. While I hid in the long grass shaded under the canopy of willows, chunky trout sidled upstream, often just a metre or two from my position in the grass, sipping the tiny pale grubs trapped in the surface film. Upstream I could see a number of trout doing the same thing. On that summer afternoon they had concentrated in the heavily willowed section of the river. Around the next bend I found the angler casting without success at a fish which rose close to his fly. Like the man I spoke to earlier in the day, he was from Scotland, and while he was enjoying his day on the river he hadn't hooked a fish. It was his first experience of trout taking willow grubs, so I bent down and watched the water for a few moments before managing to scoop one of the tiny worm-like grubs from the surface.

'They're taking something that tiny?' he asked, looking with incredulity at the grub wriggling in my palm.

'They are,' I said, 'and when they're on them they can drive you to distraction.'

142

We looked through his fly-box but he had nothing as small as a willow grub. He did, though, have a dry fly that was about the same pale green as the willow grubs, so he tied it on and went back to the fish that rose every few seconds. I walked on thinking about the slim chance he had of hooking one of these fish, but I imagined he wouldn't forget his day, casting in that avenue of willows at so many trout.

Beyond Lorne Peak Station I followed the river where it briefly hugged the highway to Kingston, the sound of the traffic drowning out the song of the river, until the river and the road parted company close to the entrance to Fairlight Station. Near the Fairlight bridge I sat beside the river and looked upstream at the purple-grey peaks of the Eyre Mountains and the monumental valley the Mataura had carved out of the land. For decades I had looked west from the highway towards the source of the river, and I had flown my Cessna through the area once, but I had never been into it on foot. I recall the envy I felt when Dad said he had been there once: I assume it was when he worked on the telegraph lines in the area back in the late 1940s. It was the only piece of the Mataura that had remained a mystery to me, and I felt exhilaration at being close to it.

The wind died and a few clouds formed around the summit of Eyre Peak as I made my way west along the river's now open, rambling course. JD was to meet me in an hour, although I felt I could have carried on walking into the night, buoyed by knowing how close I was to the headwaters. It had been a day of easy walking through the dry late-summer landscape, profiled towards the end by the clean cut of the light.

Around six I left the river close to the confluence with Robert Creek and walked out to Cainard Road where JD picked me up.

Back at the Brown Trout Cafe that evening, a man sat on a bench near us and looked our way a couple of times before saying, 'Where are you boys from?'

'Dunedin,' I said, but quickly added that we had a place in

Balfour and had been fishing the area for thirty or forty years, wanting to add to our credentials as locals of a sort.

He looked close to seventy, lean and handsome but worn by sun, cigarettes and life. He narrowed his eyes, as though the smoke from his cigarette was irritating them, but I saw in them a look of interrogation. 'You know Bob Toffler?'

'No,' said JD, after a brief hesitation.

'Do you mean Doctor Bob?' I asked.

'Yeah, Doctor Bob. Old friend of mine.' Doctor Bob is a retired radiologist from the United States who spends most of the southern summer in Balfour fishing, which is how we met him. 'I'm Sam. Mind if I join you?'

'Sure,' I said. 'How do you know Doctor Bob?'

'He used to stay with us at Riverview when he came out fishing, years back. It's his birthday tomorrow. I'm heading down for a surprise party.'

A couple of drinks later we found ourselves calling Doctor Bob to wish him happy birthday for the next day, and while the phone was being handed around it occurred to me Riverview was almost certainly the property I had so much trouble getting through the previous day.

'Had trouble getting through your property yesterday, Sam. Felt like I was trapped in a prison for a while, it's so well fenced,' I said.

'Environment Southland forced us to put in all that fencing. Some of my mates who fish it tell me how bloody hard it is with all that growth inside the fence.'

I decided not to tell him what I thought about the no-trespass signs along the road, and what looked like a strategy to keep anglers off the river, partly because he leases the farm to others who might be responsible. The issue of access is made more complicated with the recent intrusion of commercial interests and the attempts by some to monetise the value of the river.

Sam invited us to join the Athol Fishing and Hunting Club,

which we happily agreed to, figuring that it would be a fine thing to belong to a fishing club based in a small town beside the river.

Back at the campground in Athol we jokingly warned two couples from the Czech Republic who had moved into the unit beside ours about the thinness of the walls, and the risk of my snoring keeping them awake. They laughed and said they had the same problem in their group. In the slowly fading light, we stood on the deck and talked with them about the river and fishing for the trout that lived in it. They had walked upstream from the camp earlier in the evening, casting little imitation trout and metal lures at trout. 'We saw a few great fish, and some followed our lures, but none would take. It was a beautiful evening for a walk, though.'

'It's too low and clear now for those lures. You need to be here in the spring, when the river is higher and slightly murky. Right now the trout see too much,' I said, although my last experience fishing that way was almost fifty years earlier, so I felt far from an expert.

JD snored lightly, and similar sounds came through the wall from our neighbours — just light mellifluous sounds that played no part in keeping me awake. What kept me from sleep was the childlike excitement I felt at heading into the last day of my journey, and the walk that lay ahead, into that part of the river that had never felt the soles of my boots.

LAST DAY: INTO THE EYRE MOUNTAINS

Before the walk began I hoped some friends might join me for the odd day, but as I lay in bed thinking about starting the last day I was pleased to have made the journey alone. The periods of loneliness I felt turned out to be a blessing. While there were moments on the walk when I would have valued the chance to talk to a friend about what I was seeing and feeling, being alone meant my focus was on the river and the places it ran through.

As the days passed, I began feeling better about being alone, and cherished the quietness and space it allowed. I am used to the slow searching upstream with a fly rod, and the deep insights that come from the intense focus on the water when I'm looking for trout, but the experience of walking without a rod had been different. It added another layer to the things I noticed. There were moments when I felt I was seeing the landscape for the first time. At times I looked at the same tawny hills for hours on end — and in the case of the Hokonui Hills, day after day as I walked north from the coast. Once I overcame the maddening slowness of it, I took pleasure in subtle changes

146

of light and shadow on the land. I smelt the land: the odours given off when rain begins to fall on dry country; the sweet-sourness of silage; acrid cow shit; a hint of clover honey; wood smoke; damp sheep's wool; and the hard-to-define smell of the river itself, something that remained a constant — as though its essence wasn't gathered as it went but instead lay somewhere high up in the peaks where it starts. I heard the changing song of the river, and the wind that tore at me for the first days, and felt the rain on my face.

When I lay back during the regular breaks I often found myself lost in the fine detail of something like a rusty knot on a barbed-wire fence, or a dying red-clover flower nodding in the wind. Some days I watched towering clouds filling the sky like the clouds in a painting by J. M. W. Turner, altering shape and colour as I walked towards them — towards the majesty of it all, in the clear southern light. For a time, I lost interest in the world outside this valley of water, and time passed as though I was in a trance.

However, I was pleased that JD, a close friend for over forty years, had agreed to walk with me on the last day. We met in 1976, the year I returned to the south after a few years working in Auckland and London. It proved to be a serendipitous meeting. It started with a letter I wrote to Tony Orman, an angling writer and conservationist, after reading a piece he wrote about the threats to rivers. In his reply he gave me contact details for some people in Dunedin he had encountered who had views similar to his about the challenges rivers faced. He mentioned Dave Witherow, Brian Turner, John Dean, Bill McLay and Charlie Boyden, and before long I joined their group, meeting to talk fly-fishing and hatching plans to save our rivers. While I don't see much of Brian these days, I regard him as a friend, and I have fished with Dave and JD ever since. Bill became a friend and angling mentor until he died unreasonably early. Sadly, I knew Charlie Boyden for just a year or so before he drowned while fishing the Arahura River. We got behind the Save the Rivers campaign which helped galvanise support for the 1981 Wild and Scenic Rivers amendment to the Water and Soil Conservation Act 1967. Brian, Dave, JD and I joined Bill McLay on the council of the Otago Acclimatisation Society which successfully fought to have the Mataura River protected by a national water conservation order.

***

Rain had fallen overnight, but as JD and I readied to leave Athol, tendrils of mist began lifting from the hills. We stopped for breakfast at the Coffee Bomb in Garston, but it appeared deserted. A Frenchwoman who ran the furniture shop beside it told us the man who was to open it was on his way. She said that he lived on the other side of the bridge, so we walked to the river and waited. The young Frenchman cycled into view while we were transfixed by a solid trout feeding in the deep run under the bridge. He went past with a smile, and I yelled after him, 'Long black for me! We're on our way.' He looked back over his shoulder and waved.

We ambled back to the bridge, leaned on the upstream rail, steaming coffee in one hand and bacon-and-egg roll in the other, and watched the river rushing below. Its journey had just started, while mine was close to its end.

JD drove along Cainard Road into the tightening grip of the Eyre Mountains. We left the car near Robert Creek and began by climbing a steep spur covered with exotic forest. The source of the Mataura, under the shadow of Eyre Peak, lay about fifteen kilometres ahead. Patches of snow remained on the south-facing slopes, almost 2000 metres into the eggshell-blue sky. Native forest filled the upper valley, while matagouri, flax and tussock covered the drier tawny-coloured north-facing slopes. After the slow change in the landscape downstream, it felt remarkable that we had moved so quickly from the open river flats near Fairlight into the majestic upper valley. Far below our perch on the side of the track, the Mataura slalomed along the ever-tightening valley floor. We dropped down to the river, crisscrossing it as we moved upstream. The rocks I picked off the bottom were rich with nymph life. The river was all bounce and tumble, driven by the urgent pull of gravity, leaving few places for trout to evade the power of the water. A few pools were formed where the stream ran hard against spurs that reached the valley floor, and in one we found three trout — one of them perhaps a trophy — holding in the deep, ebullient flow. We have fished for these creatures for so long some might imagine we would be blasé about seeing another, but we stood, both of us captured by their wild beauty, until they sensed our presence and were lost to the deep shadowy water.

We stopped for lunch at the base of Iron Spur, beside a tributary that drained the Bowels of the Earth — a bush-filled steep-sided valley overhung by a near-vertical cirque of forbidding rock and scree that reaches 1800 metres in the north. Surprisingly, the stream that flowed out of the valley looked gentle and stable, probably because of the dense forest that protected the land from erosion.

We followed the valley as it curved south-west, with meagre tributaries joining the Mataura from the high slopes every few hundred metres. Hawks circled on the rising air, and a couple of bellbirds sang from a patch of bush. Ground-hugging red and yellow flowers angled at the sun from their tenuous hold on the valley floor, and when I stopped to turn over a few stones, brown lizards ran for cover. We mostly stayed together, talking about all manner of things, but for some reason avoiding discussion about my walk, as though we couldn't find the right way into the subject. Perhaps it was because I was embarrassed to say how emotional I was feeling about being beside the river at this final stage. Eventually JD let me walk on ahead, as if he sensed that was the right thing.

Downstream of Cowshed Hut, a stream draining a large north-facing tussock slope had deposited a fan of rock and gravel across the valley floor. Some of the rock was lichen-covered and had been there for some time, but much of the material was new, perhaps freshly torn from the slopes during the storm that had interrupted my walk.

At Cowshed Hut I looked at my map and measured the distance to the point where the Mataura became a series of creeks flowing off the Mataura Saddle and Eyre Peak, about six kilometres west. The hut was a neat four-bunker, clad in corrugated iron with a rusted roof and a long-drop toilet thirty metres away. The desiccated skull of a deer hung from a wall at the front of the hut. There were few entries in the hut-book. Most had been made by deer hunters, in there during the roar, with just one from an angler, a Norwegian, who wrote of a huge trout he had caught.

'John, I'm keen to go on a bit,' I said. 'Up to the beech forest and get into the river. I've got shells to deposit. You want to go further?'

'You go on. I'll wait here. No rush.'

'Thanks, mate. You just don't want to have to look at my naked body in the river,' I said, trying to sound light-hearted. I put the shells in my pocket and without my pack headed west, beside the river flowing through stable grassy banks on this first significant river flat. About halfway to Beech Hut I stopped in a clearing and sat by the bank. I figured that one of my best high-school long-jumps would carry me across the stream. This was far enough. I crouched beside the stream and drank the sweet water, so cold that my forehead ached after a few gulps. Sun flicked through beech leaves that shuffled in a breeze building from the west. Darts of light reached the green, grey and brown rocks that formed the base of the little Mataura. The tumble of the river was all I could hear.

I took a couple of steps into the middle of the flow and held the two sides of the cockle shell collected at the start of the walk, before dropping one in the quiet water behind a hefty rock. The symmetry of the back of the shell caught the water the way the wing of an aircraft catches the air, causing it to descend slowly in a series of little curving turns. It looked alien — cream and white against the darker colours on the bottom of the stream. I held the other half of the shell above the water, ready to let it go, but as I touched it to my lips to wish it well on its journey in the opposite direction to mine I decided I couldn't part with it, that its slightly worn edges would remind me of my walk up the river long after most of my accumulated memories had deserted me. When I had gathered the shells from the sand on the coast I thought about the cycle of water, and wondered how long it would take to transport fragments of the shells back to the coast from the mountains where I had planned to leave them. When I looked down at the light dancing off the pale shell half a metre below, my thoughts turned to my grandchildren George, Dylan, Maeve and Elliot — and, in turn, their possible grandchildren — and wondered how many generations would come and go before a piece of the shell makes it back to the Southern Ocean.

The renewal of the river in the mountains felt like a miracle, emerging from the tiny patches of snow four or five kilometres west, and from a few tarns and scree slopes, all flowing off the steep-sided mountains. The life of the river starting unblemished, like an infant. For a moment I wondered if I should go on, climbing higher, looking for something to call the source, before deciding I had gone far enough — that no matter where I stopped there would be some trickle of the river above me.

I stripped off, and with my legs numbed by cold, grasped a large rock. After taking a few deep breaths I pulled myself down until the water flowed over my head, as though I was just another rock in the current. I came up gasping, mostly from the cold, but also because of the emotion I felt about finishing the walk and the beauty I found in the headwaters of the Mataura. While standing in the current I saw with clarity how insignificant I was. Knowing I was made from the same atoms as the things surrounding me was exhilarating. The sandflies that came from the forest to feed on my blood while I dried off in the breeze had no doubt about my place in the universe. I found myself yelling into the forest like a fool.

Back at the hut JD and I had an oddly awkward embrace, unusual because we haven't found it difficult to hug each other over the decades, through times of joy and sadness.

'I've brought a couple of things with me,' JD said, smiling, as he rummaged in his pack. Out came pieces of fruit cake and a beautiful hip flask. 'Talisker.'

I found the Mochi sweets Sue had given me for this moment, and we shared the bounty sitting on the terrace overlooking the Mataura. 'Here's to the Mataura,' I said as we raised our little cups towards the river, before taking the whisky in one shot.

'Wow, that's so good,' I said, so we had another, before packing up and, following the river, heading back to the car, helped along by the breeze. Behind us, an approaching front pushed ragged grey clouds over Eyre Peak. The edge of the shell in my pocket gently nudged my leg as I walked.

THE AFTERMATH

The days spent walking, mostly alone, left me quieter than normal when I returned home, as though I had been in a monastery, and my body felt lethargic as it slowly let go of the journey.

It took me a month or two before I summoned the enthusiasm to assemble my notes and audio recordings and begin the process of writing about the trip; a task mostly completed by the end of winter in 2017. It wasn't until I had finished writing up my daily log that I was able to stand back from the details of the walk and reflect on what it had meant to me.

Some things were clear from the start. The walk was physically harder than I expected. My feet took a battering, and for a few days deeply cracked heels threatened to derail the whole venture. By the end of each day I was weary, although my fitness improved as I went along, and by the end I did feel as though I could have carried on — almost forever. By the end of my journey I could see how easy it would be to be seduced by these long walks.

With hindsight I was able to put the scale of the walk into perspective. Apart from Māori, who almost certainly followed the river part of the way south from the West Coast, I don't imagine more than a handful of people would have made this walk — mostly because few would see a reason to do so. Adventurers regularly walk the length of the country, so by comparison my journey was more like a clamber up a hill than a climb up Everest. It was, however, enough of a challenge for me as I approached my seventieth year, and it left me with a sense of satisfaction.

I learned that the river is a harder companion below Gore than it is above. The combination of rough riparian strips, few gravel beaches, hard-to-cross water, and electric fences close to the river's edge made walking the lower river a challenge. I also realised early that walking without marked tracks creates difficulties. In the lower reaches I often felt trapped on the wrong bank, and was regularly left eyeing what looked easier walking on the unreachable other side.

The walk reinforced my sense of how rapid and dramatic the modification of the landscape has been since the 1850s. In less than 200 years the land and river it flows through have been transformed from a place where the forces of nature moulded and cloaked the land imperceptibly over thousands of years, to one where modern agriculture shapes everything. The change has been like a fracture, leaving a landscape devoid of the slow saturation of human history and memory evident in the landscapes of Europe and the Americas. Many of the native birds and plants simply didn't survive the change. The extent of the modification became clear when I looked north from the south coast towards the Tuturau area. In 1850 it would have taken over two weeks to cover the distance to Tuturau, while I expected to make it in just three days on foot. By car, the trip from the coast to Tuturau takes less than an hour.

In close to 240 kilometres of river I was surprised by how few people I saw near the river: perhaps only twenty anglers, and most of them were north of Gore. Anglers were the only people

I saw near it, and none of them were children. When I was a boy the river around Gore was used as a playground, but during the time I walked it no one else paid it any attention. A couple of times a year now I see families picnicking and swimming by the river, but they weren't around during my walk — although with some of the weather I experienced I wasn't surprised by the lack of swimmers.

In my early years on the river my recollection is that most anglers were to be found near Gore, and on the lower river, towards Wyndham, while the upper river was only lightly fished. That picture has been turned on its head in recent years, with fewer anglers on the lower river than before, and many more upstream of Ardlussa — an area which, when I first knew it, had a backcountry, deserted feel about it. The change reflects changes in the way we live. The anglers I see now have more time for recreation than before. Roads are better, cars more ubiquitous, and long flights — once the domain of the few — are now accessible by the many. Queenstown, just an hour's drive north of the upper river, exemplifies the rise and rise of tourism. Tourist anglers flock to the area to fly fish, and the upper Mataura, because of its proximity and beauty, is right in their firing line. I understand their motivation, but am concerned at the impact the popularity of this upper part of the river is having on the angling experience. Even in this distant corner of the planet, solitude is becoming harder to find.

When the area was first settled by Europeans the river was treated as a convenient drain, a view that was common when I knew the river back in the fifties and sixties. Attitudes have changed, but only slowly. The major towns on the river, Mataura and Gore, set their backs to the river as though it wasn't seen as a thing of beauty when the first English and Scots settled in the district.

The fencing of the riparian strips beside the Mataura has been impressive, particularly downstream of Gore. I did feel, though, as I trudged my way through the tangle of growth that has taken hold in that space, that the riparian strips have created an opportunity to replant native species — to assist in holding the banks together, as well as creating a place for birds to flourish. It could form a long green belt from the coast to the mountains, slicing through the monotone landscape of intensive agriculture, but currently few appear to care about these strips of land.

POSTSCRIPT

On the first day of 2019, I visited the river downstream of Cattle Flat with Dylan and George, my oldest grandsons, aged six and nine, respectively. I pitched our tent in mid-summer grass, close enough for us to hear the murmur of the river as it accelerated down a ripple before slowing into a deep pool. The backs of sheep were visible above the long grass close to the tent; sleek black cattle bellowed at us from a distance. Copious spring rains had left the land and all that lived on it looking fat and soft. The late afternoon was warm and the land glowed as the sun dropped below the thin layer of high cirrus; the ranges to the north were cut with purple shadow.

For the first time in close to sixty years I threaded a worm onto a hook, and showed the boys how to lob it slightly upstream so it would settle in the depths of the pool. We watched the rod tip for action while we built a fire on the gravel beach. After the initial fierceness of the fire subsided, I wrapped potatoes in foil and covered them in embers. While the boys painted mud masks on their faces, I cooked sausages and baked beans over the open fire.

They climbed on willows, so high at times that Dylan got

stuck and I had to help him down. Back at the rods the boys waded into the river, touching the line, sometimes believing they could feel a fish nudging at the worm. While inflating the boy's air-beds I could see George wind the line in and manage to lob the worm back into the depths of the pool. I'd been telling them to leave the worm resting on the bottom and wait for a trout to find it, rather than keep winding it in. They were impatient after a couple of hours without a bite, and I watched unsurprised as George immediately started to wind the worm slowly back towards the bank. As I was battling to get the plug into the bed I heard George yell, 'I've got a fish, Pop!' His rod was bent under the weight of something.

'You sure it's a fish? Might be the bottom,' I said.

'It's a fish, Pop! See, the line's moving upstream.'

'Let me check,' I said, before holding the rod and feeling the solid weight of something. Just when I was convinced he was snagged on the bottom, I felt the pulsing weight of a trout. 'It is, Georgie, it's a fish.' I tightened the drag on the reel and handed the rod back to him.

Dylan grabbed the net and waded in until the water reached the top of his shorts, as though he had been landing trout all his life. For a long minute the big fish used its weight and power to stay in the depths of the pool, before it lunged upstream at the very moment George was trying to wind it in. The knot I had tied didn't hold up under the strain and the fish broke free, taking with it the hook and a piece of line, along with our hopes and dreams.

In the last of the day's light we melted marshmallows over the embers and ate the squelchy, sometimes charcoal-coated sweets. 'Don't tell your mum and dad, but let's clean our teeth in the morning,' I said as we made our way to the tent. I read just two pages of Dylan's book to them before we were too tired to go on.

'I can't believe I lost that fish,' said George.

'I know, Georgie. It's the second trout you've hooked and lost. Perhaps tomorrow it'll be third time lucky.'

I woke as early light flooded into the tent. Dylan, who was having his first night away from his parents, snored lightly beside me. George turned towards me and opened his eyes. It felt like a miracle that we had got through the night undisturbed.

'You want me to read you some of *The Odyssey*?' I whispered. He nodded, so I clambered over the sleeping Dylan and began reading from an illustrated edition of Homer's tale of adventure. George's eyes showed that he was captivated by the story, and I read on for half an hour, savouring this not-to-be-forgotten moment — reading Homer, accompanied by the sound of the Mataura as it slid south, while tucked up in a tent with two of my grandchildren.

'Who are your best friends at the moment?' I asked.

George looked at me with a smirk, and said, 'My iPad.'

'Really,' I said, chuckling.

'You know Thomas, he's one,' he said.

JD arrived unannounced as we were clambering from the tent. He had guessed where we might be camping. 'I woke early, before six,' he said. 'Knew I wasn't going to get back to sleep. Thought I'd try to find you, see how you were getting on.'

The boys gathered wood for a fire they insisted we needed. While I brewed coffee, George picked up his rod and began to wind the reel. 'I've got one! It sure is a fish, I can feel it,' he said. We scrambled to the bank and stood with George as he pulled on the fish. Surely this one will stick, I thought. Soon the fish appeared in the shallows, and while Dylan hovered near with the net, I said, 'Just pull it onto the gravel, George. It's a beauty.'

George had indeed caught his first trout. A three-pounder, which we kept, because he simply couldn't let it go. I smacked the fish on the head while the boys leapt around me in excitement. For a time they wouldn't put it down, as though holding it was the only way to make it real.

'We need to keep it cool, so it doesn't spoil. Put it in the shade and lay some grass over it,' I said, but I knew how they felt and understood their need to touch and hold this magical thing.

'They look like naturals,' said JD, holding his coffee and smiling at the boys.

Over the next hour George caught another and Dylan reeled in two. They put the fish over their shoulders and walked around with them, and when they were eventually placed in in the shade, they sat with them, touching their flanks and soft eyes, and feeling their teeth. 'They've got teeth on their tongues,' said Dylan. They ended up with blood on their trousers, and scales and fish slime on their T-shirts.

'Look, Pop, if I push on the eye I can turn it right around,' said Dylan.

'Can I take one home? I want to keep it in my room,' said George, eyes glowing with excitement.

As the warm westerly blew around us, I stood for a moment, transfixed, watching the boys sitting with the four trout, touching them, while the river rolled past. The vision took me back to 1953, beside the same river, when I sat beside the first trout I caught, touching its soft eye. It felt like the closing of a circle.

A couple of days later I showed George a black-and-white photograph of me as a baby in the Mataura River, up to my shoulders in the water, with Dad standing over me.

'Look, Pop, that's the same place we were. See the willows on the other bank, and the deep hole, and those branches sticking out,' he said.

'It looks just like it, Georgie, but it was downstream of our camp. Not too far away, though.'

In the freshness of his seeing, he immediately spotted the emotional similarity of the places. Towards the end of my walk I felt I too was seeing the river with a new set of eyes — perhaps as a child might. I was struck by the magic of it as it snaked its way through the landscape. Walking stopped me thinking about the past or my future, and in the process the quality of my own seeing improved.

***

When I was growing up in Gore the area felt unambiguously my place. I found it hard to imagine any other. While I've grown closer to the river over the years, I've also developed an understanding that has made me less certain about claiming it as my place. Like the trout that played a part in drawing me to the river, I have a growing sense of my position as a late-comer. The reading I did before the start of the walk played a part in that. The shallow roots of human connection with this landscape are inescapable. It has left me feeling part-alien, part-local.

The river has played a role in defining my life. That it's been a one-sided relationship is of no consequence. All that matters is that I have loved it, and made largely unsuccessful attempts to protect it from harm. In return, it has given me a lifetime of pleasure and shown me a way into the natural world.

By the time I finished walking I felt I had experienced the land and river through my body — with my feet, and legs, and back, as well as with my eyes. In *The Living Mountain*, Nan Shepherd wrote that 'the thing to be known grows with the knowing'. Her insight echoes my experience with the Mataura, and the landscape it flows through.

PART TWO

My first experience of the Mataura — with Dad watching over me.

THE START OF THE AFFAIR

My affair with the Mataura started with a baptism of sorts. It was my second, and is the only one I believe in now. The moment of my dunking was recorded in a photograph taken by Mum. I'm up to my shoulders in the river, staring back at the camera across the current and stones of the riverbed. Dad stands over me, head down with his hands on knees, looking at his first child. The photograph is taken on a warm afternoon in February 1950. I've just turned one; Dad was a young man not long back from his brief stint in the war in the Pacific, and while his life had only fifteen years to run, our evening by the river isn't tarnished by that unknown.

***

Mum arranges to meet Dad for tea by the river. She makes sandwiches of buttered white bread, slices of silverside, lettuce and pickle, and fills a bottle of goat's milk for me. The pram sags under the weight of it all as Mum pushes me along Lawrence Street on our way to the river. On our left we pass bungalows surrounded by gardens, and stark, new State houses on the right. It is before the optimism of small towns in the south erodes, and Gore's expanding.

It takes less than ten minutes to reach the flood-banks and gravel road that leads us the last few hundred metres to the river, into another world of backwaters, rough paddocks, and a narrow dirt path under an avenue of willows that takes us to the bend in the river. The air smells of willows, weeds, and the damp organic odour the Mataura has sucked from the land as it winds its way from the Eyre Mountains to this place called the Bend on the north side of town.

The pram lurches as its narrow wheels cut a path across the gravel beach on our way to a patch of shade. Mum lays me on a rug dappled by sunlight fragmenting through leaves that shuffle above me. It is the first time I hear the sound of the river as it rushes over a broad ripple upstream of our picnic spot, before slowing with a sigh into a deep, tree-shadowed pool beside us. On the far bank a rope, used by grown-ups to swing out over the middle of the hole where they let go and crash into the river, hangs from the willows, its frayed end catching the flow. I am spellbound by the light, the smells and the sounds.

Dad cycles down the dirt path, leans his bike against a willow trunk, removes the clip from his trousers and joins us on the rug. Others come to this place beside the river, families like ours from East Gore, to swim, picnic and fish.

Dad takes off his sports coat and shoes, rolls up his trousers and shirt sleeves, exposing his white Southland skin, and carries me into the river where he sets me down in the current. Mum calls me and I look back at her kneeling on the gravel at the edge of the water as she clicks the shutter on Dad's camera. While Mum dries me on the rug he dives into the deep hole and thrashes against the current, then hobbles towards us across the hard gravel, his hands rubbing his face red. He boils water for tea in the Thermette and they eat sandwiches while I sit on the rug drinking milk. In the still evening air mayfly imago leave their temporary homes in the grass and willows, and dance in front of us as they dip their egg-laden tails onto the water. Soon the long glide below us is pockmarked with expanding rings left by trout as they sip the spent insects from the mercury surface of the river.

**

By the time I was five I was so drawn to the river that my parents and grandparents felt they had to tell me outrageous lies about the dangers I would face if I dared to cross the flood-bank alone. For a couple of years I wasn't game to disobey them, but I did hide in the long grass on its top and look down into the green algae-covered backwater, searching for the crocodiles and snakes they never fully convinced me were waiting for a little boy like me. All I saw and heard were ducks, frogs, wading birds and rabbits, and they drew me closer to it all.

We lived in a triangle bounded by rolling hills to the north and east, the Mataura to the west and the Waikaka Stream just three blocks south. It was my playground. I dug up rabbit holes, collected birds' eggs, fished for eels, perch and trout, and raced my trolley down the gorse-patched hills. Cousins, aunties and uncles lived over the bridge; my grandparents lived between our place and the river. We didn't have a car until I was well into primary school, so our physical horizons were narrow. I began life in a semi-detached State house, before we moved next door to a house I lived in until I went to university in Dunedin. This small part of the valley was almost all I knew, and for me it was unremarkable apart from the river that flowed through it.

For most of my life I have remained connected to the river. I walked over the bridge into town several times a week when I was a boy, mostly to go to the weekend matinees. After the movies I would dawdle back over the bridge eating oysters and chips wrapped in newspaper, while counting the trout hovering behind most large rocks. During my five years at high school I biked over the bridge four times a day and at times saw the river so thinned by drought that it looked possible to hop across it without getting wet feet. I remember leaning over my handlebars into sleet and snow while the thunderous river hurled bloated cows and trees at the shuddering bridge and threatened the existence of our town.

My deepest connection to the Mataura, though, has been when walking its banks, rod in hand, searching for trout. I still recognise pools, ripples, lignite and rock seams from my days walking the river as a twelve-year-old when I drifted worms through its pools and retrieved spinning lures through its bouncy runs. The river connects me to my closest, most enduring friends. It is an intimacy that started in 1950 when Mum wheeled me to the river, and it has been reinforced by memories of love and happiness that surrounded my early years near it.

WAIKAKA STREAM

I have been drawn to quiet secluded places near water from as early as I can recall. I have a gregarious side, but there's a part of me that finds comfort in solitude. When I was a boy I loved the lonely, wild feel of the Waikaka, even though it was just a ten-minute walk from our house over the railway line behind my primary school. It was the first tributary of the Mataura River that I fished, and I never saw another angler on it, probably because it had a larger population of eels and perch than trout, but that wasn't a distinction that bothered me in the late 1950s.

The first time I fished the Waikaka I biked down the new bitumen on Wentworth Street, turned left past the primary school, crunched onto the gravel back road, crossed the railway line, and leaned my new bike into the high-summer grass. I pushed through the broom that guarded the approaches to the unused bridge, sending the pigeons that lived under it skimming away towards town. It was a warm day, but in the musty shadowed air under the bridge it felt cool. I stacked my gear bag beside the dark beams and looked into the water. Upstream the banks were choked with willows but below, where it flowed through Hamilton Park, they opened a little. Under the bridge the water was still, more like a pond than a stream, and the bottom was muddy. Blue and red damsel flies hovered and darted over the surface, invisible frogs croaked, and water-boatmen sculled in the tea-coloured water. Tadpoles, black and round, some with tiny rear legs, hid in the weedy edge of the stream. The narrow space between the bridge and the rising ground it butted up against felt like my own cave. Beyond the bridge, green hills rolled away to places I could only imagine.

I had a short spinning rod and a Mitchell reel that I bought from Smith and Rainsford's with money saved from my paper run. I landed the black-and-gold lure into the water under the overhang of grass on the far bank. Rays of sun bounced light off it as I wound it, wobbling, towards me. It had travelled only a metre when the first perch darted from the peaty depths of the stream. The perch held behind the lure, waiting for another chance to grab it. When it passed close to the rotting wooden bridge pile in midstream, more perch, with red fins and vertically striped sides, joined in. As I was about to lift the lure from the water one charged in and was solidly hooked. It came ashore with a flick of the rod and landed in the long grass. I stood over it, stunned that I had caught it. At first it flopped about, then lay still, its black eye staring at me, its mouth gulping strange air. Light shone through the translucent red fins, and the spiny dorsal fin sat erect over the bronze back and quivering striped flanks. I had been told they were bony, not worth eating and it was too beautiful to feed to the hens, so I slipped it back to the stream. The perch lay still in the water for a moment before darting into the dark pool.

I cast the lure again and again, probing different areas of shadowed water. Perch chased the lure for a while, but by the time I had landed three or four they lost interest, and eventually I couldn't find a fish that was willing to join the game.

It was time to try something new, so I took my eeling line from the bag. It was a simple thing, just a few metres of thick twine wound in figures of eight onto one of Dad's garden sticks, a couple of metal nuts for the sinker, and a thick-shanked hook. I broke the shell of a rotten egg on the bank and let its stinking contents leak into the stream, pushed a chunk of rotting meat onto the hook, unwrapped a few metres of line, swung the hook and sinker a couple of times to build momentum, and lobbed the bait into the middle of the hole beside the bridge pile. I sat on my haunches and pulled the slack out of the line, watched it sink to the muddy bottom and waited. It wasn't long before I felt the tentative pull of an eel. Eels tug and tear at the meat rather than gulping it down, and I knew that I had to wait before trying to set the hook. Eventually the line pulled away across my finger. I jerked it back and felt the weight of the eel, churning and twisting, as it made for the snags around the bridge. Eventually I dragged the long black eel from the peaty depths, head facing me with its body spinning wildly. The eel twisted up the line as I dragged it from the water onto the bare earth under the bridge, where its slimy body was quickly covered with mud and dried leaves. I bashed it on the head with a rock many times before it was quiet enough for me to drive the blade of my sheath knife into its tail to finish it off.

My excitement at seeing the eel appear from the deep water was replaced by panic at how long it took to die. For a moment I sat with my heart pulsing in my ears, then I stood on its head and used a stick to pry the hook from its mouth filled with backward-sloping teeth. The eel's slime dried on my hands and legs, eventually flaking off like the skin on an old blister, but the sweet-sickly smell remained. I landed two more and added them to the sack lying in the cool shade of the bridge. It was time to go home and show off my catch.

The train whistled a warning as it screamed towards the crossing, steam and smoke blasting from the black engine, the face of the driver looking at me holding my bike as they flashed towards Gore, towing red carriages full of blurred faces from far-off towns — faces that looked back at me, standing a few metres from the train, holding my wet sack of eels. The uniformed guard waved and watched me cross the still throbbing lines before I climbed on my bike and cycled home. As I turned into Wentworth Street I passed the wooden villa where my great-grandparents on the McDougall side of my family had lived decades earlier. Their house was only a couple of hundred metres from my fishing spot. I never knew them, but I had been told their stories by my grandmother. My great-grandfather, David McDougall, worked in a Glasgow shipyard when he was twelve. They came to New Zealand young and poor, and my great grandmother raised thirteen children while he became a Member of Parliament. He was a friend of John A. Lee, someone Gran told me was important. Gran and Pop lived just a block to the west, and our house was a couple of hundred metres north. My world was confined, and close.

When I got home I built a fire on a bare part of Dad's vegetable garden, and when the embers glowed in the breeze I threw on the eels before feeding them, still steaming-hot, to our white hens who pecked the flesh, stopping from time to time to lift and cock their heads to the side, sharp red-ringed eyes staring, as though disbelieving their good fortune.

I returned to the Waikaka Stream often during my primary-school years. I almost always went by myself. It was at the wild outer edge of my everyday life. I bought a three-pronged spear, attached it to an old broom handle and wandered the banks of the stream looking for eels to spear. Once in a while I crept up on little trout finning close to the bank, hoping to tickle them. I managed to touch a couple, but wasn't able to slip my hand up their flanks and insert my fingers into their gills.

I was at high school when I last fished the Waikaka Stream. By then I was a sprinter, and some summer evenings I went to Hamilton Park, beside the stream, to practise sprints, jog, and be entranced by the long legs of my friend Wendy. She was a fine athlete and a beautiful young woman (soon to become Miss Southland), which played no small part in my keenness to train with her. On some of those warm evenings I saw trout rising in the sinuous runs between the water plants, but for a year or two my mind wandered from the fish.

The Waikaka Stream has changed since then. The old back road has become State Highway One, and many of the willows that once lined the stream have been removed. The rolling hills to the south, which felt like a boundary to my world when I was ten, now look unimposing. The trout, perch and eels probably remain, but the wildness that existed when I was a boy looks to have gone, although I wonder if I was a boy again whether I might still find magic there. I was lucky to have experienced the Waikaka, because when it mattered, it was my wild place where I could dream and feel space, quiet, and the natural things that connect us to our place.

EELING WITH JESSIE AND MORRIE

I have no memory of Mum leaving the house or why Dad told me I was being sent over the road to stay with the Corries. I was nine, and I imagine my parents didn't think I'd understand what was happening. My younger brother and sister were sent to stay with Gran and Pop. Mum was pregnant, but that wasn't talked about much — it was a time of well-intentioned secrets and lies.

We had lived opposite Jessie and Morrie Corrie since I was a baby. As soon as I was old enough to cross Wentworth Street by myself I visited them to sit in their tiny kitchen watching Jessie bake cakes, or help her collect warm eggs from the nests of hay at the back of the hen house. They had a pet pig, Pedro, delivered by some hunters that had shot its mother in the hills west of town. We carried him buckets of food scraps and wet mash that smelled like sweet porridge. Pedro gobbled it all in seconds. I leaned into the sty while he ate, scratching his hard skin and black hair that was tough as a broom.

Some Sunday mornings most of the adults on our block would gather in the Corries' front room to talk, laugh and drink beer from the flagons Morrie had collected a few miles beyond Gore's dry boundary. I collected cash from the men and walked to Vercoe's corner store to buy the yellow-and-pink-covered sports papers. When I returned I sat on the floor and watched them talk and laugh. Once, Morrie got Dad into a wheelbarrow and wheeled him over the road while they both roared laughing. The Corries didn't have children, and treated me like one of their own. They were kind, funny and adventurous, and I loved spending time with them.

'How about we go eeling tonight?' said Morrie when he arrived home from work on my second day with them. 'Been a while since the hens have had a good feed of eels.'

We packed the car with sacks, lamps, a couple of gaffs, a rug, and the picnic tea Jessie had made. Morrie was big, round-bellied, and his old car leaned towards him as he stepped on the running board to get in. With his slicked-down hair, parted just off the centre of his head, and his pear-shaped body, he reminded me of Oliver Hardy from the movies I watched at the St James theatre.

Morrie let me push the starter button on his car. 'Give it some more tittie, Dougal,' he said as I pulled the choke knob, blushing.

'Great, the river's at a perfect height for those rocks,' said Morrie as we crossed the Mataura on the Gore bridge. A line of gulls sat on the sewage pipe upstream of the bridge, and once in a while they lifted off the pipe and glided downstream before turning to face the current, hovering over the river as they searched for passing morsels. Everything was fat below the sewage pipe — birds, eels and trout, fed to bursting.

We turned onto the gravel and headed south, beyond the fellmongery towards the second sewage pipe, close to the hospital, where we left the road and lurched across a paddock to the river and the shade of willows. The air smelt heavy with animal waste from the fellmongery and the chemical-laden flow from the half-pipe as it entered the river — a smudge of grey, slowly lost as it mingled with the water.

The river below Gore is about as broad as it gets, and seams of rock and lignite run across it, creating a series of shallow ripples and holes. The rock has been sanded into a smooth imprint of the water by silt and gravel, washing down from the mountains in the north since the last Ice Age.

Jessie laid the rug on the bank and we sat in the shade of willows, eating sandwiches and cold pieces of oxtail. They drank beer poured from a ceramic flagon, while I drank cordial. When it finally got dark, Morrie pulled on his black thigh-waders and stepped over the first of the rocks. He faced downstream, straddling rocks, over a narrow gash of water — gaff in one large hand, lamp in the other. Armed with my flashlight and gaff I followed him out onto the rocks. I teetered on the edge of balance, watching every surge of current, hoping it would be an eel sliding upstream, drawn to the beam of light. Jessie sat close to the bank, under the wobbling canopy of light from the lamps.

The first eel showed as nothing more than a grey flickering shadow in the current. I ripped the water with the gaff, but felt nothing as the tail of the eel disappeared upstream. 'Good sign, Dougal. They're on the move,' said Morrie.

He soon had one which coiled up the handle of the gaff as he scrambled on tiptoe from rock to rock on his way to the bank. I missed another before I pushed my gaff down the smooth rock to the bottom of the channel, and held it there while I waited for another chance. Before the next eel slid into view I had a sense it was coming. The water rushing between my legs had a tumbling rhythm that I became used to, and the first hint of the eel was a minor change in that sound as the water was moved by the fish. When the eel swam into the beam of light I ripped the gaff up into its belly, and after taking a couple of greasy steps I was on the bank, dropping it into the sack.

We caught eels into the night before Morrie slipped as he

scrambled towards the shore, taking me with him into the smelly current. The eel on his gaff slithered away over the top of our flailing bodies, before we made it to the bank. Morrie thought it was funny, but it did mean the end of eeling for the night.

'Don't want you to get cold, Dougal,' said Jessie as I huddled on the rug with a blanket around my shoulders while Morrie drained water from his waders. My clothes smelt of eel; that sickly sweet-smelling slime that dried like another skin.

After the commotion of falling in, there was a moment of quiet. When I turned back towards them I saw that Jessie had stopped smiling. She glanced at Morrie who stood under the willows, on the edge of darkness. 'Dougal, a couple of days ago your mother had a baby girl,' he said, in a tone more serious than I had heard from him. 'They didn't want to tell you at the time, because she wasn't well. They weren't sure what was going to happen. She died this afternoon. They called her Sally, and your Dad said she was beautiful. Mum will be home soon, and you can go home then. Do you feel okay?'

'I think so,' I said. It felt like the right thing to say, because I was the oldest in our family, and I didn't want to cause a fuss.

'You'll be all right,' said Morrie.

I woke in the night in a bedroom that didn't feel familiar, and clung to the bed, heart thudding in my chest, until I worked out where I was. My family felt scattered, and I wanted us to be back, living over the road at 26 Wentworth Street.

In the morning we made a fire in the garden and tossed the eels on the embers. When their black skins wrinkled and curled away from the steaming meat we forked them onto the wheelbarrow and fed them to the hens and Pedro. The hens picked every speck of meat from the bones, leaving only the curved spines on the dusty floor of their run. Pedro ate the lot, bones and all.

In the afternoon I saw Mum arrive at our house in Gran

and Pop's car. From Jessie's front room I watched her get out and climb the steps to our back door. Our house was quiet when I entered. Mum sat on the good sofa in our front room, her face pale as a dinner plate. We were back together again, but nothing was said about Sally. My brother and sister had returned. Someone asked me if Morrie and Jessie had told me what had happened. 'Yes,' I said.

Dad walked in later, angry that Mum had been brought home from the hospital without him knowing. When he flew into a rage I cowered in our front porch with my brother and sister, not wanting to hear the angry words. We weren't told if there was a funeral for Sally, and tried to go on as though nothing had changed, but it had, and for a while our house felt empty.

OPENING DAY, 1959

It was 1 October 1959, the start of the trout-fishing season in Southland, and the first day I had been allowed to go to the river without an adult watching me. I opened my eyes in the dark room I shared with my two younger brothers. I hadn't slept much but must have drifted off briefly before it was time to get up. I listened for rain before I eased my head under the curtain. I could see stars through the frosted window, and knew it was going to be a fine morning and the river would be fishable. My stomach buzzed. Countdown to the start of the fishing season had started weeks before. I looked forward to Christmas and my birthday, but this was like those two events rolled together. For days I had been willing time to move more quickly, and desperate to get to sleep each night, because time passed faster when I was asleep.

The luminous hands on the clock beside my bed showed a quarter to five as I slid quietly from bed and pulled on my clothes, wiped sleep from my eyes, and eased quietly into the kitchen. The coal range had slumbered through the night, leaving the room warm as I gulped down a glass of milk. In the laundry I put on my oilskin parka, woollen hat and gumboots, checked the can of worms collected the previous afternoon, and picked up my fishing bag and rod. I was on my way by five. Frost sparkled under the street lamps as I turned into Hamilton Street to meet my friend Jimmy who waited in the dark outside the front of his house. I was scared of his house, and meetings outside his front gate suited us both.

I had promised to be home by eight that Thursday morning, to give me time to clean up and have breakfast before school. Until that summer my trips to the river had been illicit affairs, with friends or alone, and against the stern instructions from my parents and grandparents, who had seen in my young eyes the magnetic attraction the river held for me. Their threats hadn't stopped me exploring the willowed banks of the Mataura, skimming stones, floating make-believe boats of dried wood down its ripples as I bombed them with stones. I played mock battles with friends among the willows and broom that edged the river near Gore, but I feared my father's steaming temper so I hadn't been game to take my fishing gear from the house. By 1959 either I had worn my parents down or they had decided I could be trusted to go to the river without them.

Before the cloak of winter left the Mataura valley I took the money I had saved from my paper run to Smith and Rainsford's on Main Street to buy spools of nylon, shiny lead sinkers, hooks, swivels, and a small green fishing tin to hold it all. It was a shop for serious fishermen. I lingered over the wooden compartments holding flies, some stiff and upright, others with fine swept-back wings, and ran my fingers down the smooth cane rods on display. I had watched our neighbour, Mr Cunningham, using a fly rod, and several times stood on the Gore bridge high above a man swinging flies across the trout I could see finning in the current, sometimes darting towards the fly before settling again close to the riverbed. The fisherman cast and swung the flies several times before taking steps downstream where he repeated the process. Once in a while his rod would bend and a trout would flash towards the deep water surrounding the bridge piles, bouncing into the air as it went. It looked an improbable way to catch fish, and anyway my pocket money wouldn't buy that sort of gear, but I was captivated by the image of the line slicing through the air.

Jimmy and I turned off Hamilton Street and exchanged bitumen for gravel as we crossed the flood-bank and cycled north in a pale light rising over the hills in the east. The air was so cold I had to give my freezing hands turns in my pockets. Beyond the road end we headed down a narrow track, scaring rabbits as we went. The cold air smelt of gorse, broom flowers and wet wool from the sheep we heard coughing and shuffling on the other side of the gorse hedge. We left our bikes leaning against the wooden fence that separated the farmland from the wild edge of the river, and pushed through the last line of willows before crunching onto the shingle banks of the Mataura which curved, under a sliver of fog, through the ripple above us, before slowing into the pool we were to fish.

I pushed a forked willow stick into the gravel to hold my rod, attached a sinker and hook to the line, and impaled worms onto the hook before making an angled cast upstream. The sinker landed with a splash just above a drop-off, where fast bouncy water rushed into the deep pool that looked almost black in the half-light. The rod tip jerked as the sinker tumbled along the bottom until the current ran out of energy to take it further. I set the rod down in the willow fork, wound out slack in the line, flipped the toggle on the Mitchell reel to stop the handle running backwards and eased off the drag. Jimmy was set up just a few metres closer to the top of the pool. We stood with our backs to the low sun, hands in pockets, eyes flashing between rod tips and the point where the line entered the water, searching for a tightening of line or tapping of the rod tip.

Jimmy's rod bent first. We stood over it, willing another telltale bounce. It nodded again, before the rod bent heavily and line peeled from the spool. Jimmy lifted the rod and tightened into the trout. The silver fish held off in the current for a time before Jimmy walked backwards and hauled it bouncing onto the gravel. He smacked it on the head with a stone before we knelt beside it, touching its soft eye, pulling its mouth open to feel the needle-sharp teeth, and smelling its musky river odour. Jimmy wrapped the fish in a white flour bag and put it into his fishing bag. I wound in and checked my worms which I replaced with a fresh lot, and soon I had a trout of my own on the bank. We recast and, with a fish each already in the bag, felt free to leave our rods and explore the river.

The beach downstream had been carved by the huge bucket from the gravel plant on the opposite bank, and in the channels and holes that remained we found trout cruising. I lay on the bank and watched a trout slide by just a metre from my face, and held my breath as I looked into its eye and watched its mouth open and close on an invisible feast.

Occasionally a fish would take something off the surface, engraving an expanding circle of ripples — symbols of feeding trout that years later became one of my favourite signs on the river. I aimed my Box Brownie, clicked the shutter, and wound the film on. The trout looked huge at close range, but in the photographs all I managed to capture was sun reflecting off the water, a few weed beds and the outline of one trout looking like a tiny version of the real thing.

As I turned back towards the rods I could see only one left on the willow forks. Mine was about to leave the gravel and follow the attached trout into the pool. I sprinted to my rod and leaned back on the trout that was headed downstream. It was larger than the first — close to three pounds, and a trophy for a ten-year-old. I couldn't wait to show it off to my family. Jimmy landed another before we wound in and headed for our bikes. I biked down Hamilton Street with the trout suspended over the handlebars, my fingers through the gills, just to show the fish off in the now-busy street.

Mum sliced the trout into thick steaks, dusted them with flour and salt and fried them in butter over our coal range. Within an hour I was sitting in our classroom thinking more of trout and the river than the early lesson. My clothes smelling of fish and browned butter.

For the first couple of months of the next few seasons Jimmy and I fished the Mataura every chance we got. On school days we didn't get far beyond the northern boundary of Gore, but in the weekend we explored and fished the river halfway to Mandeville. We caught fish, pushed into gorse bushes looking for birds' eggs, lit fires on the bank to warm us before the sun came up, and dug up rabbit holes hoping to find a soft baby rabbit to take home as a pet. The rabbits never lasted long. Some died under feet in the kitchen, and I suspect Dad let some go, thinking that my homing pigeons, lamb and guinea pigs were enough for our backyard.

I never caught more than four trout in a morning during the three or four years I fished with Jimmy, but we rarely failed to catch at least one each, until December, when the river lost the last of its winter grey and, in the sparkling clear water, fish became harder to catch on the worm. Our best mornings were when the river was rising rapidly, flooding new ground. One morning I arrived at the river later than Jimmy to find that he had landed ten in the previous hour. The fish were bulging with earthworms, but by the time I started the action was over.

Jimmy and I had fishing in common, but little else to hold us together. He had few friends at school — he was small, not good at sports, and often smelt as though he had peed his pants. I hardly knew his parents, and rarely ventured inside his house. Jimmy never talked about his sister who lay on a divan in the lounge, making strange sounds, stick-thin limbs motionless, her almost hairless head rolling from side to side. I don't think I ever knew her name, nor what happened to her, and when I did go inside I stood near the door, not wanting to look in — but unable to resist. By the end of our first year at high school we had made new friends, and while we never fell out, I doubt that we spoke more than a few words to each other until I left Gore for university. I never saw him again.

The river has altered its course in places since Jimmy and I fished it almost sixty years ago, but much of it remains as it was. When I walk those sections of the river now, I recognise many of the banks and pools we fished. These familiar places remind me of my youth, fishing with Jimmy, both of us full of wonder, energy and hope.

OTAMITA STREAM

Few human footprints had marked the banks of the Otamita when the first trout sipped mayflies there in 1869. The fish liberated into the Otamita were the first in the Mataura catchment, just a year after the original ova arrived from Tasmania. No permanent Māori settlements existed in the area and the settlers from Scotland and England had seen this land for the first time only sixteen years earlier.

The juvenile trout would likely have been taken by horse and cart from the south coast over rough bullock tracks, through the new settlement of Longford — now Gore — and on to the southern edge of the Waimea Plains. The convoy came to a frontier landscape of wetlands, tussock, mānuka and matagouri; shaped millions of years earlier by a collision of plates that folded the land into the razor-back ridges that form the Hokonui Hills, and more recently by the huge river flows that followed the last Ice Age. The Otamita begins its life as a series of brooks draining peaty bogs high in the Hokonui Hills and flows east for twenty kilometres to join the Mataura River near Mandeville.

When I first saw the stream in the early 1950s, I was just a boy and I paid it little attention. We had crossed it on the plains close to where it meets the Mataura and it looked not much more than a drainage ditch flowing through sheep country.

I swam in it as a teenager. It was the first summer without Dad, and we were in need of fun that warm day in the back of Mandeville. Mum lay a rug on the bank under willows that flicked the sun in the light breeze, and set out a picnic lunch while my brothers and me flung ourselves from a rope hung from a solid willow branch into the deep pool, our ripples pushing away over the clean stream bottom.

I first fished the Otamita during spring in 1978. I walked into the lower end of the tight valley that guides it through the Hokonuis where large, dark mayflies hatched late in the morning and flew off into sharp crackling light. I landed two exquisite brown trout on a tiny mayfly nymph, both close to five pounds, and from then on I was smitten with the place. For the next twenty-five years I fished it half a dozen times a season, mostly in the spring when the mayfly hatches were at their best. I couldn't imagine a better early-season stream anywhere.

One of the opening days on the Otamita I remember best was the first day of October 1994. I picked up JD in the half-light of a Dunedin morning and we drove south, arriving at the gravel road above the Otamita valley before nine. The farmer was usually willing to let us drive down to the stream, but lambing was in full swing on this high, cold country. We parked by the gate and made our way on foot over leanly grassed paddocks to the water, staying close to the fence to avoid disrupting the anxious ewes that stood over new lambs, the yellow and red mucus of birth still clinging to their tightly twirled wool. A patchwork of light and shadow carried by the wind flew recklessly across the land.

We were halfway down the slope when we saw the Otamita curving out of the tussock-covered hills upstream. At the stream edge we scanned this old friend, looking for signs of trout disturbing the surface of the pools. Nothing moved. I lifted stones from the frigid water. Large, dark mayfly nymphs wriggled across the undersides, and caddis larvae hid in their delicate cocoons fashioned from tiny pebbles glued together.

'Bottom looks fantastic,' I said. 'These nymphs look ready to go. Bound to get a hatch when things warm up.'

'Think I'll start with a heavy nymph,' said JD.

We fished upstream, taking alternate pools while the sun began tearing holes in the clouds, frayed by the first high land crossed since they left the Southern Ocean only half an hour earlier. Partway up the first pool my leader hesitated and I lifted the rod tip to feel the weight of a heavy fish. The trout ran towards the head of the pool then headed back downstream, cartwheeling free of the water before lodging itself under a deeply undercut bank. Without elegance I followed the fish in waist-deep water, my legs and feet not yet ready, on this first day of the season, to handle the rubbly bottom of the stream. I managed to get my net under most, but not all, of the trout, which slid free and charged downstream, a load of vegetation wrapped around the leader. Minutes later I held the first fish of the season — short and thick, pulling my weigh scales close to the five-pound mark.

'They don't come better than this!' I yelled at JD. He looked towards me, poked a thumb in the air, and turned back to the water. The fish ripped from my grip with a thrash of its tail and disappeared into water so lightly stained by peat that it looked like whisky diluted with a perfect touch.

We moved slowly through some of the most productive stretches because the water was too cool for a hatch and we didn't want to miss the opportunities that would surely come as the day warmed. In its lower reaches the Otamita whispers its way over fine gravel, but here, higher in the valley, it tumbles towards the Mataura with an optimistic gurgle over shattered brown rock, so different from the river-smoothed grey stones of the Mataura. In places the stream is walled by seams of rock

187

that run parallel to the current, sometimes pushing through the surface like the back of a dinosaur. Where the rock seams cut obliquely across the current the water jostles over hard steps, taking oxygen from the air as it sings its way downstream. In every other pool we hooked brilliant silver fish, distant relatives perhaps of the first trout released in this stream well over a century earlier.

After a couple of hours' walk upstream I waited for JD who was landing the second fish he had taken from a shallow riffle two pools below me. I leaned back into high tussock still damp from the moisture it had stolen like a magician from the overnight mist. Beads of water, backlit by the sun, worked their way down the leaf blades to replenish the stream. The chest-high tussock that nodded over the banks shaded the water, keeping it cool during summer as well as filtering out sediment before it clogged the stream bed. When I first knew it, the Otamita discoloured reluctantly and cleared faster after heavy rain than almost any stream in the south. The lonely sharp-backed hills and the cool, clean taste of the water helped me understand the attraction this place had for the McRae family, and others, who used local grain and this water to produce moonshine whisky in the area from the 1870s until the 1950s.

Life thrived in the near-perfect flow of the Otamita. Mayflies, caddis, dobsonflies, snails, koura and freshwater mussels grew in abundance, and the trout that fed on them were usually large, heavy-shouldered and red-fleshed.

JD leaned his rod on the tussocks, took off his vest and sat beside me. 'What a morning. What did you get, seven or eight?'

'About that, I think. And no one else here. Magic, really.'

We ate lunch with the sun warming our faces: boiled eggs, sardines, a bread roll with cheese, and an orange for me.

'How do you think the rugby will go?' I asked. Otago, with one of its best sides in decades, was challenging Canterbury for the Ranfurly Shield. It was the first time we had been contenders for the title longer than we could remember.

'In with a chance, I reckon,' said JD.

The pool we watched over while we ate lunch was about fifty metres long, and deep along most of the far bank. Opposite us the stream flowed beside a low rock cliff and it was here that a section of the current deflected from the main flow and curled back upstream into an eddy. 'I can see some duns in the foam,' I said.

Flecks of foam followed the seam of current downstream, but enough joined the rotating eddy to form a revolving carpet on the surface. Mayfly nymphs making their journey from the stones at the head of the ripple were sometimes caught in the same twist of current. Instead of extending their diaphanous wings and floating for a moment before taking to the air without the hint of a practice flight, climbing in an arc towards the tussocks, they were pulled into the foam where they remained trapped like flies in a web.

Trout don't waste energy when they feed, and during this early phase of the hatch they mostly remain close to the head of the pool in the fast ripply water, near where the nymphs start to drift. They look for concentrations of food, and the duns trapped in the foam was another spot where food could be tracked down without the need to expend much energy.

'There he goes,' I said, a dark snout sucking a hole in the foam as the trout took a stranded mayfly.

'You have a go at him. I'll head up to the next pool,' said JD.

I tied on my little dun pattern and slid waist-deep into the pool. My breath slowed to near stand-still while I waited on the snout to poke through the foam again. A short cast was all that was required, and I had made it from this same spot many times before, but the challenges involved made the outcome something of a lottery. Where I stood the water was almost slack, but between me and the edge of the foam a fast line of current tumbled past. The patch of foam rotated slowly anti-clockwise, which made picking the likely direction of the trout difficult. To allow the fly to hold in the foam long enough for the trout to gulp it down a pile of slack line had to land on the fast-moving water between me and the trout.

My first cast wasn't good enough. I waded as close to the foam as I dared and cast again, landing the fly in the foam while a series of curves in the leader fell onto the fast water. Moments before the fly was ripped away from the foam the trout took it. The big trout tore downstream, pushing holes in the water as it jumped in a blur of silver and spray. It pulled the scales at a little under six pounds, and as I held it in the water before its release, I felt the same sense of wonder I had as a boy entranced by the wild beauty of trout landed on early mornings before school. As I get older I find it harder to dodge the conclusion that we have a common trajectory and are in this game together, and that my enjoyment is in a way an unwarranted intrusion on another life. We need them, but they are indifferent to our fate. I don't feel any sense of triumph over the fish — just gratitude for the peace I find in the places fishing takes me, and awe at the beauty of the fish.

The hatch of large, dark duns gathered pace through the afternoon, and trout took them as though this might be their last supper. Two or three rose in most of the good pools as the stream danced down the valley. I landed my last two for the day in a high-sided deep pool, the fly drifting down a seam formed where two fingers of current joined close to a rock wall. Both trout lay just under the surface feasting on the passing duns. To take, they tilted upward, bulging the current back upstream for a second before my imitation tipped into their open mouths.

I had been lost in the river and the immediate moment for much of the day, my eyes searching the stream, trying to read every nuance of the water, watching the pīwakawaka and swallows and looking for telltale signs of fish. Nothing much else entered my mind. On days like this I read the water as I imagine some read sheet music — totally immersed.

JD startled me from the bank. I hadn't been aware of him sitting watching my last few minutes. It was time to go if we wanted to catch the last of the rugby.

'We should make it for the last half an hour,' I said.

'Better be worth it,' said JD, 'leaving the water with the hatch still going.'

I made a short burst forward and made the best attempt at a sidestep I could make wearing waders and fishing boots. 'I've got a good feeling about this game. Jeff Wilson has just gone over in the corner, I can feel it,' I said as I propped again off my right foot, and leaned forward to the ground, imitating Wilson making the touchdown.

JD grinned at my foolishness. 'What a day,' he said.

'Extraordinary. If there's a better early-season stream any-where I want to know about it.'

We checked into our room at Croydon Lodge, the grand name given to the hotel that was built on a patch of land once farmed by my great-grandparents. I turned on the TV and we sat on our beds with a beer while the game flickered into life. Otago was so far ahead that my premonition about the result looked on the mark. This made the slow squandering of the lead that took place over the next twenty minutes all the more painful to watch. We were still ahead with two minutes to go, but the inevitable happened. Richard Loe, who was no stranger to the wrong side of the rugby laws, grabbed the ball that had squirted out the back of the Canterbury ruck and sucked it back into the melee. The referee, who was disinclined to see this act, penalised the Otago captain who had been about to swoop, quite legally, on the ball. Andrew Mehrtens kicked the penalty and Canterbury won by two points. The day, which had started so well, was now in tatters.

'Fuck it,' sad JD. 'Let's go and have a meal.'

We trudged across the vast bitumen car park towards the

restaurant, thinking that a good bottle of red might improve our outlook. It didn't, so we had another, but even that didn't elevate our moods.

'You know, we've been opening the season together for eighteen years,' I said. 'Feels like yesterday, though, that first time.'

'Imagine another eighteen years going that fast,' said JD. 'We'll be in our sixties. Old bastards.'

'Christ, that really cheered me up. You want another drink?'

'No, let's head back to the room. I'm stuffed,' said JD.

The car park had filled with Falcons and Holdens while we ate, as though half of Gore had turned up. 'Car park's full. What's on?' I asked the receptionist as we walked towards our room.

'A male stripper's putting on a show,' she said, pointing to the bar entrance. 'It's pretty wild in there.'

'You want to go in?' said JD, laughing.

'Nah, let's get some sleep.'

Back in the room I was about to turn off my bed light when the car park burst into life. Tyres squealed, women yelled and glass shattered. Another Saturday night in New Zealand. We heard some raucous yelling down the hallway followed by a discussion outside our door.

'This is the bloody room,' a woman said. Our door shook with the heavy knocking that followed. We looked at each other without saying a thing.

'We know you're in there,' said another slurred voice.

'Are you going to get that?' I whispered. 'That stripper must have mentioned our room number!' JD didn't move.

While we waited the talk outside became increasingly crude. 'Yara bloody poofter are ya?' someone said from beyond the door.

'What do you think?' JD whispered.

'I'm not calling reception,' I whispered back. 'They'll think

192

we're pathetic. Can't deal with a bunch of randy women.' JD climbed out of bed, crept to the door and yelled, 'You've got the wrong room. Bugger off. The stripper conned you.'

This didn't have the desired effect, and the noise built in the hallway. 'Come on out, ya wanker. Show us your gear!' a woman yelled.

I turned off the light, pulled the blankets up over my head and hoped they would leave. About half an hour later they were gone, leaving a fading trail of obscenities behind them. It was well after one in the morning, and we had planned to be away fishing by seven.

I'm not sure if it was the squealing of tyres or the gravel hitting our window that woke me around five. I lay for a moment, trying to take it in.

'Just let us in,' I heard a woman say from the car park, more pleading than threatening this time. I leaned over and opened the curtains just a crack. The car bulged with women while some stood below our window, still in their rumpled Saturday-night clothes, mascara running, and big hair now frayed. Dawn touched the edge of the eastern sky. I sensed they wouldn't last long so I crept back to bed and waited for the start of the new day.

'What an opening,' I whispered. JD turned over, grumbled and went back to sleep. I thought of the male stripper, probably sleeping quietly in another part of the hotel. Cunning bastard.

EPILOGUE

For thirty years I fished the Otamita as though it was my secret stream. I rarely saw another angler fishing it, and I liked it that way. It remained a brilliant fishery for the first twenty years, but it was clear by the turn of last century that its glory days were over.

By the mid-nineties the pace of land-use change in the catchment of the stream accelerated. At first the change was mostly visual. The tussock that swayed in the relentless spring winds that blow over the south was burnt and ploughed to make way for ryegrass and clover. It started in the lower end of the valley but within a decade the burning had worked its way into the headwaters. The land close to the stream was first to change, but before long the tussock was removed from all but the high, bony backs of the hills that framed the valley.

Ditch-diggers sliced through the gullies, water soaks and swales; kilometres of tiles were dropped into the resultant scars; and before long all that remained of these valuable sponges were slight indentations in the new pasture. Where water once seeped slowly into the stream from these wetlands it now either gushes from tile drains during rain or fails to flow at all when the rain doesn't come.

The last fragments of native vegetation that huddled beside the stream were often burnt along with the tussock, and the flaxes that thrived on the banks were eaten and smashed by cattle. In places the ploughs and discs reached to the stream's edge, as though leaving any of the old landscape would be a sin. Increased cattle numbers broke down fragile banks, and their excrement found its way into the stream. Some riparian fencing was established, but usually after the burning and ploughing, and, in the unwanted strip of land thus created, broom and gorse flourished. Left alone the broom might have allowed some healing of the banks but periodically it was sprayed and burnt, leaving the strip as a sooty wasteland.

The stream now floods more quickly during heavy rain, carries more suspended sediment, takes longer to clear after high flows, and runs lower and leaner during dry spells. The increased sediment load smothers the insects that feed on the stony bottom, and the trout and birds that have thrived on them suffer. This once-great trout fishery can still produce good fishing, but it is a shadow of what it was when I first knew it.

A few anglers were the only people that really cared about

the Otamita, but in the end they had no power to stop or modify the changes that took place, while the public bodies that had the power to influence outcomes averted their eyes to what was happening. The farmers who generously allowed us to cross their land simply followed the established path of bringing more land into production. The stream was seen more as a boundary between properties — a cheap fence — rather than an integral piece of the landscape.

It wouldn't have taken much to save the Otamita from the worst effects of the land-use change. Careful protection of the tussock and native plants twenty to fifty metres from each bank and a willingness to leave some of the soaks and swales in place would have been enough — but nothing much was done, and, in the end, no one was prepared to pay the price to save this gem.

FORTUNE CREEK

Even in the five years I was away a picture of the Mataura remained with me, allowing me to walk its banks and see the piled clouds and hills that guided the river through this valley of water. When I returned it was mostly to be with family, but the pull of the river and the southern landscape was strong. I came back with a better understanding of the place, of just how special it was, but also with a knowledge that it wasn't the centre of the universe. The frigid storms that sweep up from the south remind me just how lonely and close to the slippery edge of things this place in the south is.

When I came back from working in Auckland and London, I felt the return of 'all the old feeling' that Nick in Ernest Hemingway's story *Big Two-Hearted River* experienced when he looked into a stream and saw trout after years away. I needed to be back where I knew the water and had a sense of how to fish it. I fished with Uncle Ernie when I returned. He had slowly moved from being an uncle to a fishing mate. I wrestled with him on the lounge floor when I was five, he was there on the first day I caught a trout, and we worked together at the Southland Farmers Co-op when I was at high school. The trolley I raced down the hills around East Gore, the hutch for my guinea pigs, my pigeon loft, and many of the possessions I loved in the 1950s came from his skilled hands. After Dad died, he didn't need to step in to fill the gap — he was already there. Ernie wasn't a fly fisher, but he had the fishing bug bad. Most of the time he fished a threadline set-up using metal lures, usually Glimmys and Tobys in silver or black and gold, but when the river was discoloured he was happy to sit on the bank and try a worm. Even though he lived in Gore and owned a car, he fished only in the main stem of the Mataura. I suspect the EH Holden he bought new and kept spotless for twenty years played a part in the roads he was prepared to use.

***

I opened the season with Ernie for a number of years in the 1960s and 70s, before meeting fly-fishing friends in Dunedin. We started each day in the dark, something I rarely feel the need to do with a fly rod. When we got out of the car he would arrange a pinch of tobacco on his palm before tipping it onto a rectangle of tissue paper. He then rolled it carefully, licked it shut with the tip of his tongue, twisted an end, and stuck it to his lower lip. He would cock his head to the left, cover his lower face with a cupped hand as though he was hiding something, and light the smoke with the flare of a wax match. After he coughed we were ready to crunch over the frosted grass, steaming breath and smoke curling behind us in the blue half-light. We usually caught a fish or two each, but rarely more — four or five was a big day. Most were caught early, before the sun inched across the valley floor to the river. We kept all of the fish we caught. He wore a working man's cap over a grey cow-lick, an oilskin parka and black-rubber thigh-waders, and netted his fish with a fold-out net holstered on his belt. He didn't waste time dispatching trout, dropping them straight into his shoulder bag, still thrashing.

Our best days were early in the season when the river was full and milky blue with snowmelt, and our leanest when the sun shone and the river was low and clear. Often on those sparkling days we came across trout in the shallows, backs pushing water as they took drifting nymphs. We caught one or two on a lure swung through them, but mostly we just chased them off.

I found Fortune Creek on one of those season-opening mornings with Ernie. We parked near where the creek entered the Mataura, and hadn't paid much attention to the backwater we crossed on our way to fish the broad ripples and runs of the river. By mid-morning I had four trout in my bag, one of my best days ever. I caught my fifth where Fortune Creek joined the river. It wore different colours from the fish I had caught in the Mataura. A dark-olive back with exaggerated black-and-red-haloed spots on flanks tinged with a butter yellow. The operculum had a patina of chrome.

'What are you doing?' said Ernie as I began to return the fish to the water.

'We don't need it. Thought I'd let it go.'

'Don't be silly. Some other bugger will catch it and they won't put it back.' It would have been the first keepable trout I had returned, but I whacked it on the head and watched it quiver as the life drained out of it. Ernie didn't really like eating trout, but it was a time before much thought was given to the fragility of the natural world, so all the trout above the size limit were kept — and in Ernie's case, mostly given away.

'Let's have a beer,' he said, lifting two bottles of Speights from the cool water. He flicked off the tops as though this had been a regular thing, and we sat drinking, mostly in silence, our eyes drawn towards the Hokonui Hills that had formed a backdrop to all of Ernie's seven decades. Our experiences had seen us headed off in different directions, and we struggled to find a language that would bridge the gap. Halfway through the bottle Ernie's look changed. A humorous glint developed in his eyes suggesting that, given half a chance, he could slide off the rails. It felt time to gently rib him.

'Those new teeth look mighty fine,' I said.

'Got me into a spot of bother, those teeth. They had better look good,' he said, smiling. 'Got a spare set now. Thought the old ones had gone for good, down the toilet. Bloody shock when Ngaire found them behind the couch. Wouldn't have been quite so bad if they hadn't been sitting in dried vomit, eh. Still would have been in trouble, though.'

'Bugger. Not many women shift the furniture every week to do the Luxing,' I said.

He lobbed his empty beer bottle into the willows on the edge of the creek. After a moment's hesitation, mine went in the same direction.

When we returned to the area a week later I explored the creek while Ernie fished the river. The spring water of Fortune Creek entered the Mataura unpromisingly through an unstable backwater formed by the shifting gravel of the main river. There was limited cover, and I didn't see a fish until I reached the willows. Under their canopy the creek changed. The clean, pea-sized gravel on the stable bottom looked as though it hadn't moved in a decade, and green-and-bronze water plants shifted in the current like flags in a light breeze. Trout held in the thigh-deep avenues that formed between the weed and in the small indentations scooped out by the current. Large trout swung in the current, the white of the inside of their mouths showing as they lifted in the flow to feed. The water was cool and clean. Cased caddis clung to the bottom, snails fed on the weed, and water boatmen lived in the slack water on the edge of the creek. I had read about spring creeks, but this was the first I had seen. It was tight, closed in, and the trout were so near when they cruised quietly along the edge I had to press back into the vegetation and hold dead still as they went by. They were close enough for me to look into their searching eyes.

I didn't have my fly rod with me, but I did have one of the first flies I had tied. It was a simple thing consisting of a few turns of lead under a body of brown seal's fur and a tail of hen hackle. At the time I tied it I thought it was just a simple start, something I would quickly go beyond, and I did, but simple as it was it would have been good enough to catch most of the trout I ever encountered. Mallards flapped off a section where a short backwater branched away from the creek. A deep weed-choked hole marked the intersection. A couple of arteries of current pushed through the weed into a pocket of clear water about a metre across. As I watched, a large trout pushed through a gap in the weed and hung suspended in a shaft of light in the open water. It swirled after a couple of water boatmen before it left the clearing on one of the threads of current. I cut the lure from my line and tied on the tiny nymph. It wasn't heavy enough to cast, but as I was only a couple of rod-lengths from the opening I thought I would be able to lob it into the gap. There was a push of weed before the trout glided into the opening. The trout spotted the nymph, and tipped on its nose as it followed it down — but it didn't take. The second time around the nymph landed on the water as the trout appeared. It took my imitation and I lifted the rod to feel the heft of the fish, tightened the drag and hung on. For a moment things went my way. The trout crashed out of the water and landed prone on top of the weed. Waist-deep in the current I managed to touch it with my net, before it flopped back into the water and headed downstream, the line heavy with weed, and broke free.

The visual intimacy that came with fishing a fly captivated me. It was the last time I used my threadline rod. It was also one of the last times I fished with Ernie. His bandy legs had started to give out on him, and I could see in a look on Aunty Ngaire's face that said she thought I was keeping Ernie out on the river longer than was good for him. His house in Gore overlooked the Mataura, and in the days when information on the state of the river wasn't as ubiquitous as now, I would call him to ask what the river looked like. From then on, I rushed past his house eager to get to the river without delay. While we kept in touch, I regret that when he could have done with some company, as he sat by the river using a worm as an excuse to be there, I didn't find the time to be with him.

For the next fifteen years Fortune Creek was my secret water. I fished it three or four times a year. It changed very little, apart from being shortened by a hundred metres when the Mataura leaned on it during a huge flood in the 1980s. I went with another angler on just a couple of occasions, and only once saw a stranger on it. 'Tough,' he said. 'They don't call it Sucker Stream for nothing.'

The fishing was always a handful, and four was the most I ever landed. Usually it was just one or two, and once in a while I wasn't up to catching any. I know it helped me as a fly fisher. I almost always found fish to cast to; all sight-fishing, in polished, unforgiving water. It usually took three or four hours to cover the best of the creek. Beyond that it separated into a number of threads running through open country. Trout, hidden at the base of flax bushes and willows, lived a long way up these tiny slivers of water.

Fortune Creek lay near the heart of the productive land that was converted to dairy farming in the 1980s and 90s. Sheep farming wasn't sustaining the farmer who generously allowed me to cross his property to fish Fortune Creek, and I sensed that he was a reluctant convert to dairy. Fortune Creek suffered quickly. The water lost its clean gloss, and I stopped drinking from it. It became choked with weed earlier in the season than before, and the flow diminished. Cows broke down its banks upstream of where I fished it, and the dips and hollows that held trout gradually filled with silt. The trees and flax bushes that shaded and cooled the water and created the indentations that held trout got in the way of centre-pivot irrigators and were removed, converted into plumes of smoke in the autumn sky. The pūkeko and many of the other birds that inhabited this place went along with the loss of cover. A community of life gone before it could adapt. Only the mallards stayed in numbers.

Fortune Creek didn't contribute much to the flow of the Mataura but, along with a number of other small spring creeks, it had been there for centuries, running steady and cool, helping to keep the river alive. I fly over the area often during the fishing season and still see these shining fingers of water, but too often they are stripped of vegetation, channelled and bridged to allow for the wheels of the irrigators to pass over them as though they didn't exist. Diluted cow shit arcs through the air to fertilise the land and all else that gets in the way.

I didn't fish Fortune Creek for the next decade but a few weeks ago, Dave landed us in his aeroplane on the beach near where Uncle Ernie had parked the day I discovered it. I walked up its banks a short distance and quickly felt that it was like looking at a friend, once young and beautiful, but old now, close to the end. I landed a trout near the confluence with the Mataura, but after covering only fifty metres gave up following this old love. I sat on the bank of the creek, thinking about my days here decades earlier with Uncle Ernie. He is long gone, and the creek is a shadow of what it once was.

Aldo Leopold published *A Sand County Almanac* in 1949, the year I was born. The lessons aren't new. As he watched the marshland of Manitoba disappear, he wrote, 'Some day my marsh, dyked and pumped, will lie forgotten under the wheat, just as today and yesterday will lie forgotten under the years. Before the last mud-minnow makes his last wriggle in the last pool, the terns will scream goodbye to Clandeboye, the swans will circle skyward in snowy dignity, and the cranes will blow their trumpets in farewell.' I was reading Leopold around the time Fortune Creek was close to its best, feeling we wouldn't make the same mistakes, as though we were above that sort of destruction.

LIES AND BROWN BEETLES

It is increasingly difficult to get us on the river early these days. That the Balfour group are all pensioners has something to do with it — this move towards old age which came at us imperceptibly at the start, before embracing us with the usual irresistible maladies. It's lucky that most of the time it isn't necessary to be on the water at dawn, and the hatches we pursue now conveniently occur in the middle of the day. Autumn mayfly hatches and mid-summer willow-grub falls are perfect for the slackening pace of our lives. Some hatches, though, demand an earlier start than we are used to: mayfly spinners can lay their eggs in the middle of the day, but the best falls often take place around dawn and in the still air of evening, while brown beetles tend to bumble and fall into the river during the balmy nights of early summer. Dawn is the time to target trout taking them.

Dave in particular has a finely tuned dislike of early starts. He isn't that enthusiastic about fishing in the evening, either — reckons it gets in the way of eating, drinking and debate. He operates in a different time zone from the rest of us. He is often without a watch, and has managed to set his internal clock in line with Perth, in Western Australia. I'm not sure how he decided Perth would be the right time zone, but it fits him like a glove. He happily sits up until two in the morning then reads for an hour or so, before stumbling out of bed around ten, or later if nothing much is on. If he is forced awake before eight it's hard to get a civil word out of him. I find silence is the best approach on these rare mornings. As long as he can catch fish around the middle of the afternoon he's happy, but if he has a week or so when the days get a bit hot for great fishing and he starts hearing stories about anglers catching fish early in the day he falters, and once in a while speculates about the fish we might be missing out on by sleeping in.

***

JD and I arrived in Balfour early evening. Over dinner Dave told us that the fishing had turned tough — too bloody hot — but he had heard of a bloke who caught lots of fish during an early-morning spinner fall. One of the best he had experienced, apparently, and close by. The thing that pleased Dave about this story was that the spinner fall didn't start until around nine, and the numbers of trout out slurping them down just outweighed his reluctance to make an early start. He agreed that we should give it a go, and when we left his place around midnight we hoped he would take the hint and hit bed early.

JD and I woke around six, and over coffee decided that if we waited until nine to get going we might miss the hatch — and besides, it was one of those magical January mornings that almost demanded that we get to the river. The trick would be to get Dave going before the hatch died. We were beyond simply buggering off and leaving him sleeping, because if we experienced the hatch we hoped for, he might not forgive us. We decided that the lesser evil would be to tell him a well-intentioned lie.

JD was the natural choice to tell the lie because he has a more convincing line of banter than me. 'Okay, Dave, time to get going. It's just after eight. Here's a coffee. We'll be away in fifteen minutes. Beautiful day, and we don't want to miss that hatch. Dougal will cook breakfast when we get back.' Dave took the coffee without a word, although a dazed scepticism about the merits of what we were doing crossed his face.

We parked under willows not far above the Ardlussa bridge. It was a warm, still morning, the mountains to the north pushing into a sky that at the horizon was pale peach before rising to eggshell blue. No wind ripples broke the mirror surface of the long pool that stretched above us. Perfect for a spinner fall.

We sat on the grassy bank at the bottom of the pool watching the odd splashy rises from small trout, expecting the more measured sipping of monsters slurping spinners to start anytime.

'If it's going to happen it'll be here,' said JD with the sense of certainty he often has about fishing spots. I was starting to doubt that, and thought that even if the rise did take place, we might feel crowded on this one pool, so decided to walk upstream beyond the bouncy ripple at the head of the glide. As I passed the ripple I sensed rather than saw an alien tilt of water. No flies were hatching, and it wasn't a place to find trout taking spinners, so I tied on a Royal Wulff to explore the water. On the third drift over a deeper seam in the flow the mouth of a trout cut through the surface, and the fly disappeared. In the fraction of a second when both trout and angler knew the connection between them was real, the fish hurled itself into the air, throwing a curl of backlit spray like a dog shaking water from its coat. I looked downstream as I landed the fish, and was certain that Dave had seen what was happening, just fifty metres above him. I waved and sped past the pool above, before landing several more trout in the next ripple. The fishing was about as easy as it gets, with little of the casting precision required when trout are taking spinners or willow grubs. On the brown beetle the trout often sit deeper in the run, giving them a larger window of vision — allowing them to range across the flow to pounce on the hapless beetles, drifting without hope of lift-off. I hurried upstream, finding a couple of trout in each ripple for close on an hour, before I turned back.

When I returned JD was casting unconvincingly at a couple of small fish at the tail of the pool, and Dave — well, he was sitting on the bank looking disgusted.

'Nothing happened here,' he said. 'No spinners, and apart from those minnows Two Pies is casting at, I haven't seen a thing. Absolute waste of time. How did you go?' I could tell from the look on his face that it he wasn't ready for the truth.

'I landed one just above you taking brown beetles,' I said. 'Thought you saw that. I waved at you. Got a few more upstream. All in the ripples.'

'Really,' he said. 'Bloody useless here. Last time I'll be on the water that early. Let's fuck off.'

We didn't have the heart to tell him what time he really got to the river until we were heading back to Balfour and his spirits were lifting at the thought of coffee, eggs, baked beans and bacon.

'You bastards,' was all he could manage. I doubt he'll hit the water early again in his life. It was a beautiful summer morning, but it wasn't a time to raise the compensating benefits of being up early to experience the start of such a fine day. He hadn't caught a fish, and it was too early for him to be awake. Nothing else mattered.

***

I am still attracted to fishing the brown beetle. I look forward to warm November nights when the hard backs of the beetles clatter against the window, and by morning lie floating in the dog's water bowl. They fly like lumbering bombers, and wouldn't stand a chance against birds if their raids were conducted in daylight, so their search for vegetation takes place in the dark. In the pre-dawn cold, enough of them fall from their leafy perches, and if they happen to be over water they land with a plop of substance. Trout focus on their heavy landings, and eat them in the dark until their stomachs can't hold another.

The best places to find trout taking beetles are the small creeks and tributaries of the Mataura that flow through the bucolic Southland farmland. There I cast my Royal Wulff into the tight little seams close to the grassy edge of the runs and pools, places where the trout know the drowned beetles are concentrated by the currents. The fly isn't the most accurate representation of a brown beetle, but I like it because they take it as though it's the real thing, and the tufts of white act as a lighthouse for me on the dark water in the dawn light. All of the large fish in these creeks are on the lookout when beetles are about, and they show themselves with bow-waves and swirls. They take without guile and throw themselves into the often misty air, fish that are preposterously large for water that even as an older bloke I can sometimes leap across. Richly spotted trout, with yellowed flanks, fat, and strong in the cool water. The takes are usually languid in keeping with the time of the day, and the sense the trout probably have that the beetles aren't about to fly off.

The fishing gets harder once the sun touches the water. When the trout slide under the overhung banks and into the depth of the pools, it's time to walk back to the car with the last of the mist rising from the land, past the burly lambs leaping on the stream banks suggesting they too feel the freshness of the morning. Time to head the old Land Rover back to Balfour, and coffee, breakfast and an hour on the bed with a book.

SPRING WIND

Only eighteen days into the new season and I was impatient with the weather. Spring in the south is usually boisterous, changeable, but this year the tempests that have lanced the Southland plains have been unusually venomous. New grass has been tossed and flattened by freezing wind, and willows flayed with such verve the streams are littered with shredded branches. Winter arrived like a guest who on first meeting appeared interesting and fresh, but who eventually drank the last of the whisky, started braying obnoxious rubbish, and finally wouldn't budge. The small rain-fed tributaries of the Mataura that I enjoy fishing in the spring have been stunted by the elongated cold. They are low this year, lean as the scrawny bum of an old man.

JD and I drove to Balfour early in the second week of the season. We have been taking these journeys for around forty years, and I value the conversations on the way almost as much as the fishing. A few weeks earlier we had been chasing permit (one of the great challenges of salt-water fly-fishing) in the warm water of western Cape York where our enthusiasm for facing the hard edge of a Southland spring had been blunted. Mostly we went west to see Dave, whose company we missed over the winter, and partly because the season has to be kicked off sometime and the forecasters might have been wrong about the isobars tightening. The wind that hammered and tore at Dave's place suggested they hadn't misjudged a thing. JD parked facing into the gale and we used our shoulders to open the doors wide enough to slide out. We ate late, talked and sampled single malts into the next day, reminded by the roar outside that an early start wasn't likely to be needed.

By morning the cooling air had tethered the gale; the snow-heavy mountains to the north appeared softer, and looked to have crept closer under cover of the howling night. The modest calm held during breakfast but when we stepped into the sharp morning light, frayed clouds, a thousand metres up, sailed on the blue like racing yachts headed downwind. Dave, who can fish whenever he chooses, quickly decided this day wasn't going to be one of them. JD and I drove to the Waimea without joy. He dropped me just a paddock from the stream, and agreed to pick me up at four. 'Keep your phone on. Just in case we need to change plans,' he said.

He is a man of many names. I call him John when things are serious, JD most of the time. Dave calls him Two Pies on account of his pie-eating feats, and Kevin Ireland often calls him Doctor Dean because of his inclination to view the world through the lens of a degree in philosophy. Brian Turner simply calls him Dean in a way that is vaguely endearing, but might not be, depending on the circumstances. JD has avoided new technology (fly rods aside) since I have known him, until he turned up with this 'smart phone'. I wondered if he knew how to use it.

Within twenty metres I sensed this wasn't a normal spring. No contrails from fleeing trout rippled the surface of the stream, and no fins or snouts betrayed feeding fish. I hugged the willows on the western bank seeking shelter from the nor'west gale that poured over the Waimea Plains. It is a wind that starts somewhere in the Tasman Sea; our spring wind. As it approaches the West Coast, the isobars are squeezed tight by the Southern Alps that stand in its path, pushing it up and sucking the moisture-dense clouds dry, before hurling it, torn and bucking, towards Southland.

Thirty minutes went by before I saw the first trout. It was suspended mid-ripple, behind a rock in water just deep enough to cover it, and should have been an easy target, but the wind made landing my tiny nymph on a track towards its nose close to impossible. The big fish was curiously inactive, occasionally swinging in the current but only to dodge willow branches drifting in the stream. I cursed as I stumbled downstream to retrieve my fly from a willow branch that taunted me by flailing like a hooked trout as I tiptoed to reach it. As thoughts of walking up behind the trout and giving it a swift kick started to surface, it moved fractionally and took my nymph. The trout rolled and headed downstream as though stuck in first gear. I lifted its ghastly head onto an overhang of grass edging the stream. It was broadest just behind its eyes, the dull yellow-hued flanks sloping away into a mean underfed thinness. I should have whacked it on the head because it was beyond recovery, but I couldn't do it so slid it back into the stream, hoping nature would do what I wouldn't.

My phone rang. 'I can't fish in this gale. Saw a couple but it's pointless,' said JD. 'I'm headed back for a milkshake. I could pick you up if you're done, or I'm happy to come back later. Call me when you've have had enough.'

My enjoyment had gone, but a little hope remained so I decided to stay. Around two, a few mayfly duns lifted from a short stony run under an overhang of willows. They climbed free of the stream in the settled air in the lee of the willows before they were captured by the gale. A couple of swallows chased them in the calm air, but even these beautiful fliers gave up when the duns were vaporised by the wind.

I sat in the reeds and long grass that lined the bank and ate an apple as I searched for trout. Swaying patterns of sun and shadow played across the stream bed. A trout rose under an overhang of willow at the top of the short run, largely hidden from sight, but exposed by the tiny ripples that pushed upstream from its nose before they were lost in the tangle of branches. Another pushed a tenuous bow-wave under the willows near the far bank, and in the crazy dancing shadows below I saw the olive back of a large trout holding still, like a piece of sculpture, while all else was on the move. Every minute or so it rose. It ignored my tiny mayfly nymph, before doing the same to a deer-hair emerger and finally my no-hackle dun. There wasn't a realistic shot at the trout at the head of the run without putting my fly line over the closer fish, but I threw the dice and landed the fly just above the nose of the top trout. It pulled out of a tentative rise at the same time as the fish I had lined bolted for cover, taking another that I hadn't seen with it.

I left the shelter of the willows and under a sky wiped clean by the gale followed the stream as it curved east where I almost stepped on a mallard crouched in fear with her young. She cackled off into the paddock in a stumbling dance, while the ducklings hit the water and sent a couple of trout scurrying for cover. I did land another in the next pool but it also lacked the sheen and heft I expect from this rich stream.

I lost concentration, energy and heart all about the same time. My cast lost its shape and accuracy, and the mayflies appeared to have made a collective decision to delay their fragile penultimate flight for another day — they get to make only a couple of flights in their brief period with wings, so they had my sympathy. While we humans begin our downward trajectory before the start of our teenage years, mayflies finish their lives with a glorious flourish, renewing themselves twice in the last couple of days, adding wings and a fine beauty to allow them to end their existence in a flurry of sexual encounters and a death that comes quickly, unsullied by memory loss, loneliness and extended decay.

I grabbed my phone and pushed the start button to fire it up but the screen stayed dark. It took a moment to accept that the battery was dead and my options were unattractive. A half-hour walk back to the roadside in the gale, but then what? A long walk to a farmhouse hoping to find someone in and willing to let me use the phone, or a two- or three-hour walk back to Balfour. A long walk in the wind, wearing heavy wet boots and waders, and carrying a rod, had no appeal. I took the lazy option and decided to wait in the hope that JD would eventually come and find me.

In the rough margin between the road and sheep-manicured paddocks I took off my gear and pushed my way under a canopy of tussocks, lay back with my hat over my upturned face and listened to the wind. With my eyes closed I soon drifted between half-sleep and dream, smelling my sweaty hat and the musty odour of the tussock and grass as I left my hard reality. This drifting place, the smells, the sun playing through the tussocks took me back to another time — when I was a boy. I had walked into the country beyond the end of our street in Gore carrying a tent, some food and a map. I had been alone, looking to earn a Cub badge for map-reading and camping. I remembered the wildness of it, the damper I cooked beside the road and the sense of melancholy I felt then, and which I still embrace with disturbing ease. I woke to the sound of a skylark overhead and looked at my watch. Close to an hour had passed. A bounce had returned to my body, and I thought how rare it was to have an excuse to take a nap, in the long grass, beside a country road. It is too easy to be seduced by comfort to think this would be a worthwhile thing to do, and there is a Calvinistic ethic here in the south that frowns on this sort of time-wasting.

I heard a vehicle approach from the south and was surprised when it stopped opposite my shelter. I didn't think it would be JD, who would arrive from the north, so with embarrassment I climbed out of the tussocks and approached the car. The driver was on the phone, and was looking away from me when I gently tapped his window. I expected shock from him but got instead a slow head turn and a nod. He wound down his window when the call ended. I explained my position and asked, 'Any chance you're headed near Balfour?'

'Could do,' he said. 'I need to find some fuel in Lumsden, so Balfour wouldn't be a problem. Put your gear in the back.'

JD was on his way to get me when I arrived back. 'I did get one of Leonie's milkshakes,' he said. 'Then I lay on the bed and slept for an hour or so. I'm finding these late nights too tough. I woke with a start. Thought you might have been calling for a ride. Then started to worry that I had got the arrangements wrong, so decided to head down to find you.'

That evening JD said he had earlier spoken to Greg, one of our local farming friends, about the wind. Greg reckoned this spring was feeling like a year back in the sixties when it blew all summer. Thirty years ago this would have washed right over JD, but he worries more about the world now. 'We might need to fish further afield to get away from the gales,' he said.

Dave and I thought this was a great idea, and immediately started planning a trip to Kamchatka, on the eastern edge of Siberia, where the weather was bound to be better.

LAST DAY WITH DES

Since the mid-seventies I had been loosely connected to Des by a love of fly-fishing and rivers. It was winter now, cold and mean, just a few months after our last day on the river. I sat towards the back of Saint Bernadette's church in South Dunedin listening to the priest talking about Des's recently completed life, and the choir that he had belonged to singing in his memory. I don't believe in an afterlife, so while the priest spoke with certainty about Des's place in heaven, my thoughts drifted to our last day fishing together, and the first day he fished, and wished I had asked him about it — when he was a boy, with never a crack in his heart.

As I had picked him up that mid-April day his tall frame seemed more bent and empty than when I had last seen him, but he was raring to go with an expensive new rod and reel bought for the occasion. While I checked the Cessna and stowed our gear, I looked back to see him smiling, looking as though he wanted to be a boy for just one more summer. It was late in the day and the Takitimu Mountains in the west were fading into a haze of bruised purple as I banked the plane over the Mataura and lined up for touchdown on a paddock on the outskirts of Balfour.

As usual we had company in our shared Balfour bach — Greg and Terry, two local farmers who early on decided we weren't too bad; JD, my fishing mate of forty years; Peter, a trout fisherman from Invercargill; and Dave, who now called the place home. Dave had roasted a haunch of bush-shot venison with parsnips, potatoes, pumpkin and a steaming pot of frost-sweetened swede mashed with butter, cracked pepper and salt. We ate late beside a fire that threw a magical mixture of light, warmth and sound into the room while we debated just how stuffed our planet was.

'Don't worry, Des,' said Dave. 'Things might be fucked, but we're a bunch of lucky skunks, and the fishing will see us out. Tomorrow will be a great day. Have another Lagavulin.'

'I shouldn't, but why not?' said Des.

Des soon started singing old songs from Ireland with his beautiful Irish voice. Dave usually demands conversation over music, but softened by the whisky and perhaps the window the songs opened into his own Irish heart, he sat entranced, looking as if he hoped it wouldn't end. When Des finished singing he sat quietly for a moment, eyes misting, before he fell from his chair and landed in a slow crumple of long legs and arms in front of the fire.

'One too many, Des,' said JD as we helped him up.

'Might have played a part, John, but I left my medication at home. I get wobbly if I don't have it. Don't worry,' he said as we propped him back on the chair. 'I'll be fine.' And for a couple of hours he was, matching Dave story for story into the night.

'You bastards take Des fishing,' said Dave as I took him his coffee the next morning. He put his book down, propped on an elbow exposing an ivory-white arm. 'Four's too much of a crowd. I've had three brilliant days in a row and I've got plenty to do here.' Dave liked to sleep late, waking slowly as the sun warmed his room. The breakfast smell of bacon, eggs and tomatoes JD was cooking wafted through the house. We lingered over another brew of coffee but Des, who woke with a spark in his eighty-year-old eyes, was keen to get going.

The plume of dust thrown up by JD's car remained suspended over the road as we turned onto the farm track leading to the river. Seasons rarely live up to the optimistic image I have of them, despite fifty years of evidence to the contrary: soft birdsong springs often ruined by high water and freezing gales, and dry summers stuffed by fronts and tempests. Autumn, though, is my favourite season, and it rarely fails to deliver. The last of the dew, laid down by the cool night, glistened on the grass while the hard ground waited on rain. Green spring had faded through summer to gold, which was bleaching now to grey. Thistle seeds drifted like tiny balloons in the light air that smelt of sheep, dry grass and the river.

We assembled rods and attached reels and flies under the yellowing willows. Leaves like tiny gondolas fell onto the water where they pirouetted on the current before piling up along the quiet edges of the pools. Within a couple of months the willows would be bare. The eggshell-blue sky faded to a thin, luminous emptiness around the mountains to the north. By late morning the air had warmed and life was busy, building for winter. Swallows and terns made sorties over the ripples looking for hatching insects, and mobs of mallards that had left the stubble fields at dawn now dabbled in the willow-canopied backwaters.

We agreed I would walk downstream for half an hour, and fish my way back towards Des and JD, who were to fish upstream from the car. The hatch hadn't started when I turned to fish, but on the swirling edge where the fast water catches the slack close to the bank, I could see signs of trout bulging the surface of the water as they fed. The clean grey stones of spring were now burnished brown with algae. Mahogany nymphs grazing the stream bed scurried for cover as I approached.

Because the river was low and clear I extended my leader to about four metres for stealth, and the tiny nymph I attached was a tapered piece of nothingness, topped with a small tungsten bead to take it through the surface film. The water chilled my legs as I eased into position downstream of the feeding trout. My nymph landed above the closest fish, and about when I guessed it would be passing near the trout tilted upwards, just a fraction, before it settled back into the hydraulic comfort it found close to the bottom. I have watched this happen thousands of times, but the magic remains. What happened next was all instinct. The rod tip lifted and bent as I felt the weight of the fish through my fingers — that elastic resistance that keeps fly fishers coming back for more. It was a maiden fish, just less than a kilo, and silver like a sea trout, with a small head and solid shoulders. It's the kind of fish we like to smoke over mānuka chips, but it was too early in the day to keep one so I slipped it back into the water. I spent the middle of the day like this, walking past the pools, and carefully searching the ripples for feeding fish. With plenty of nymphs drifting in the current, and the imperative of winter looming, the trout fed without guile. The larger females were distended with eggs, and the older males had contorted jaws, ready for the jousting of the spawn.

I had been absorbed by the fishing for several hours, but I started thinking about JD and Des upstream, and sensed I needed to see how Des was going and allow JD to fish alone for a while. It was mid-afternoon when I pushed through the willows on the sweeping bend above the car. I saw Des lying still in the grass, his long legs hung motionless over a small terrace in the paddock. I thought for a moment that something was wrong with him and quickened my stride, but he moved as I called. He pushed himself up, patting the dust from his vest and shirt. 'I've had a great day, Dougal, but I'm struggling now,' he said. 'JD landed plenty but I couldn't get my line under control, and my sight isn't up to this fishing.'

The sun warmed our backs as we sat and talked. Des about his days on the Mataura, extending decades back. He talked of the fun he had working with Dave on the Mataura Project back in the seventies which had documented the fishery for the first time and helped secure a conservation order for the river.

'I'm happy to wait here, Dougal. It's a great spot, and I feel like a snooze. JD's gone upstream, but that was an hour ago. Why don't you fish on?' He looked as though he meant it, and I could see birds feeding over the ripples so I headed back to the river.

I waded into a long pool that flowed through an avenue of willows. Downstream, backlit by the low-angled sun, thousands of mayfly spinners dipped their egg-laden tails on the river's slick surface in a dance to perpetuate the species. The purpose of their lives complete, they flattened onto the eddies of current. Along the edge of the pool trout idled upstream, dorsal fins and tails exposed in the shallows as they sipped the dead spinners without rush. I stood mid-current and cast my spinner imitation slightly downstream and back towards the willows. After a couple of attempts I managed to drop the fly an arm's length above the fish, with just enough crumple in the leader to allow it to reach the trout's nose without any hint of drag. It took the fly as though it was the real thing. That's the job done as far as I'm concerned. The moment of deception is what I love about fly-fishing, and with the dry fly the deception is exquisite. I landed several more as I worked my way up the pool before the fall of spinners slowed, my concentration was released from the surface of the river, and I thought once more about Des downstream.

I met JD on the walk back. Des woke as we arrived, and we sat, our legs hanging over the dusty terrace. 'It was magic being by the river again,' Des said. 'Best couple of days I've had in a long time.'

As we stood to walk to the car his legs gave out and he toppled to the hard ground as though shot from behind. We helped him up, dusted off the dry soil he had collected, and made our way to the car. 'I'm fine,' he said, but we had a sense that he wasn't. In that instinctive way that people know, all three of us understood that it was unlikely we would see Des on the river again. Nothing was said of this because it would have spoiled the day.

It took both Dave and me to manoeuvre Des's large frame and tangle of legs and arms into the front of my Cessna. He was asleep soon after we crossed over the shining Mataura, and didn't wake until the wheels touched the grass at Taieri. His wife was pleased to see him home, but grumped at his carelessness at leaving his medication behind.

'Dougal, I've had the best of times,' said Des, and I'm sure he had. However, within days his new gear appeared in the For Sale section of the *Otago Daily Times*. JD didn't want to see Des shortchanged in the sale, so arranged to buy the gear for a generous price through a third party. While that was the last day Des visited the river, his rod and reel continue the journey.

As I sat in the church thinking of Des, I thought about the day we shared on the Mataura. It would be the sort of day I would like to close my fishing. A soft autumn day on the river, mayflies dancing over the water, with old friends nearby. When I closed my eyes I could see him as a boy, sitting beside a chattering stream in Ireland, rod in hand, looking forward to long summers stretching ahead.

FISHING WITH GEORGE

I'm fifteen minutes late meeting my grandson George on the outskirts of Queenstown. The river at Nokomai seduced me on the way. I had a spare hour, and both the day and the river sparkled. The river has done that to me for as long as I can remember: stolen my heart and left me like a gambler in front of a slot machine, hoping that the next pull will be my salvation. In the first hour three solid fish took my deep nymph in the brisk, clear water, but I lost myself for another fifteen minutes chasing a huge trout that nosed along the edge of a deep drop-off. It swayed and rolled in the current and gave me hope that one more cast might deceive it. It didn't, and when I returned to the world of time, I knew I was late for this most important fishing trip.

We meet in a busy car park near the airport. George, soon to turn five, is delivered by his parents, Bridget and Paddy, who will enjoy a child-free night in Queenstown. I grab a coffee and sandwich in Frankton and allow George to have a bagel covered in chocolate and sprinkles. It is half the size of his face. Some goes in his mouth, some on his face, a smear from his fingers onto the café window, and what remains into a bag for later. For the drive south he sits in the car seat secured in the back of my Jeep. Road rumble, his soft voice, and my faded hearing make for interesting conversation.

'What was that, George? I heard the first bit, but what did you say after that?' was the usual start.

We first see the Mataura near Fairlight Station. 'You know, George, the Mataura is my favourite river.'

'Do you catch permit there, Pop?' he asks hopefully, because over the years I have made much fuss about permit, my favourite salt-water fish.

'No, but it's the best trout river in the world. Well, there may be a better one, but I don't know where it is.'

'When are we going fishing, Pop?'

'Soon, but we need to find some worms first.'

We pull into Stu's Fly shop in Athol to pick up a licence for George. The woman behind the counter smiles at us without reservation, and for just a moment I feel that it is a smile for me, a smile conveying more than a pleasant hello. I blushed, but see almost immediately that her greeting is directed at the two of us — an older man with a boy, about to go fishing. George spots a photograph on the wall of a permit bitten in two by a shark. 'Look, they do have permit here, Pop.'

He tries on a Simms fishing cap. Great brand, and it looked good on him, but I know I need to toughen up. 'Maybe next time, George.'

He stuffs the licence in his pocket, and we sit on a rough-hewn bench outside the shop in the sun. Time slows as he kicks his legs under the seat and works his mouth around the bagel.

Finding worms is usually easy: a spade speared into the lawn, pushed back and forwards a few times, and out come the worms to dodge the pressure waves. Today the drought had sent them deep, or away altogether. Greg, a local farmer who finds time to cut our lawns and supply us with firewood, calls round to catch up on our plans and to meet George. Even the boards he had placed behind his woolshed as worm attractors failed to deliver. We could see from the little curving tunnels where they had been, before the land dried bone-hard. Without worms our fishing will be more difficult, requiring dexterity with rod and reel that might be beyond George.

By five, potatoes and carrots are boiling on the stove in my Balfour fishing bach, not foil-wrapped and cooking in the embers of a fire by the river as I had dreamed: a fire ban rules that out. I fry a trout kept from my morning session, along with sausages, which I think a safe bet for a five-year-old. George isn't sure about my tomato relish being good enough to have with sausages, so we walk to the shop to buy some Wattie's tomato sauce.

'Pop, I don't really like fish.'

'But George, this is a trout I caught this morning. I thought you wanted to try some. I'll dish some anyway. See what you think.'

I finish the meal quickly, hoping that my haste will spur George on. It doesn't. He looks at me with the furrowed seriousness of an adult, and eating stops. 'Pop, I will have friends in my class when I start school, but I won't know some of the kids. Joey will be there to look after me.' I first heard him mention his imaginary friend, Joey, a couple of years ago. He is a figure of comfort, and a friend in times of need.

He tries to speed up by filling his mouth with sausage. Choking looks likely, and water is required. 'You eat some of those carrots, George, and you can leave the rest.' He eats enough carrots and finishes the trout without complaint.

After dinner we drive to the Ardlussa bridge for George's first trout-fishing adventure. It is about eighty kilometres upstream from where I first fished the Mataura sixty years ago. The absence of worms calls for a change of plans. The more complicated spin fishing is our only option. He holds the rod and watches the knot as I tie on the black-and-gold-striped spoon — something I last did perhaps thirty-five years ago, just before fly-fishing became my life. I walk to the river taking in the sound of the water hissing past, and watching the patterns of light filter through clouds onto the hills in the south, while he runs, zigzags, skips and jumps along with me. I point to the lure dangling on the line. 'This is supposed to look like a little fish when we pull it through the water.'

I cast the lure across the river and wind it slowly back, to show him how it is done. Then we try to operate the rod as a team. He holds the rod while I hold the line over my finger as the bail arm is released and add some oomph and direction to the cast. The spoon plops down just short of the far bank and George holds the rod while I lean over his shoulder and turn the handle of the reel. The spoon wobbles its way towards us through the bouncing water. We are transfixed by the prospects. We do this several times. My hope fades. The river is way too low and clear for this sort of fishing. I am happy to keep going, though. I look at the sky in the south and for a moment think about Uncle Ernie, long gone now, and the times we fished together, casting spoons into the river. It is the way I fished when I became bored with worm-fishing, and wanted to walk the riverbanks, searching for trout.

We fire the lure across the river into a backwater on the far side. The weight of the current pulls it from the slack into some heavy bulging water before I have a chance to wind the reel, and as soon as I manage to feel the weight of the line I see a large trout throw itself into the air in a shower of spray. We watch and I hope for an aching second that we are connected to it, before we feel the trout hurtling downstream with the current, pulling line from the reel as it goes.

'Did you see that? You've got one. Do you feel it?'

'Wow, I can,' says George.

He holds the rod and eventually gets his hand on the reel. The trout charges across the ripple, pulling more line. The run of the fish slows as it drops into a deep pool, allowing George to reel it in. Eventually it wallows in the shallows, just a few steps beyond us.

'Do you see it, George?'

'I can! Look, I can see its big tail.'

And at that moment the trout shakes free. The pull of the fish is gone, but the trout, George and me remain frozen with disbelief — for a couple of seconds. Before we can move, the fish, which has more at stake in the game than us, slips off the shallows back into the deep water.

'You almost caught your first fish,' I say, while being moment-arily tempted to lie, and try to convince him we had actually caught it and had just let it go. I can see from his face that this approach has no merit.

'I wanted to take it to school to show my friends,' he says. It doesn't matter to him that his first day at school won't happen for a few weeks. 'Gran would have cooked it for me, Pop.'

'Perhaps there'll be another.'

I fish on while George fossicks under stones for mayfly nymphs and caddis larvae. 'Do trout really eat these things?' he asks. He finds the dried shuck of a mayfly nymph and thinks it is a fossil. 'One day it might be,' I say.

We call in at Dave's on the way back to Balfour. He recounts his day fishing in the Nokomai Gorge. George snuggles beside me on the couch listening to Dave's story of landing his little plane by the river and tussling with the many trout that fed hard in the ripples. He landed eight, and as George's eyes widen I wish that just one of them was his. He doesn't say a thing, but his eyes grow as he studies Dave. I imagine this is how he will learn about older men. It's a warts-and-all education. I modify my language a bit, depending on who I'm talking to, but Dave doesn't. His is a mix of wit, insight and profanity, and I doubt that it will hurt George a bit. I hope that what he sees in Dave is the energy that sparks from him when he talks about the things he loves.

'It's past your bedtime,' I say as he climbs out of the bath. 'Don't tell your mother you were up this late.'

'I will, Pop. You'll get into trouble,' he laughs.

I read him dinosaur stories, and tell him that the Tyrannosaurus Rex could open up the top of my car roof with its teeth as though the car was just a can of baked beans. He laughs as if this is the funniest thing he has heard in days. He asks me to leave the light on when I depart. I look in on him ten minutes later and he is asleep with his tiger warming the side of his smooth, beautiful face. I stand for a moment and think about how his body will eventually change like mine. I wonder what will trigger the lines that will one day crease his face. I hope that it will be from too much smiling.

He sleeps until almost eight, and wants to be straight back to the river. We don't hook another trout, but we do catch the lure on the far bank, and I photograph him holding on to the bent rod as though playing a fine trout. It is the first fishing lie he has been involved in, and it happens on just the second time out. He follows the tracks of an excavator and finds the high, unstable banks of gravel left behind after excavation. I look away from the river and see him standing precariously on a cliff of gravel. 'George, move back from that. The whole thing could collapse.' He wants to stay hunting the riverbank for the whole morning, but we have to hurry north to meet his mother in Kingston. As we leave he says, 'Pop, would you post me a trout to Petone? I want to show my friends.'

'Be smelly by the time it got there, George.'

He is quiet most of the way back. The bustling story-telling of yesterday has deserted him. Near Garston he says, 'I'm going to be a builder, a fisherman, an archaeologist and a pilot like you — oh, and a policeman too — when I grow up.'

'You'll be busy, George.'

'I could be a policeman on Thursday, I could be a builder on Tuesday and a pilot on Saturday.'

'Wow, that does sound like fun.'

We teach each other. I teach him how to fish, show him the knots I tie, and use words that are probably new to him like 'reel' and 'cast'. In turn he teaches me what it's really like to be a five-year-old, because my memory can be untrustworthy when stretched that far back. I can recall events from my past, but filtered through my mind now I'm no longer sure what they meant, and what I felt about them. I think we both understand that the fishing isn't everything; it is being near the water that counts. I find beauty and peace in the surroundings, but I see that for him it is different. For George it is more about the excitement; the adventure of a wild place. I listen to the river, and watch the light play on the hills and clouds, while he invents stories, finds make-believe bird's nests and hides from me in grassy hollows. He plays while I contemplate, and try to make sense out of the stories of my life.

The Mataura has shaped this landscape for 15,000 years or more, leaving signs of its past in the terraces it has cut through the land and in the layer upon layer of sediment it deposited on the plains. I sense in my relationship with George a laying down of my own past, and a connection with the only grandfather I knew, Pop Hicks. Perhaps because my father died when I was sixteen, my relationship with Pop was the longest and most nourishing I had with an older man. I think of him as I try to build on the layers of my relationship with George.

WHY I FISH

There were three of us, access points were limited, and we had one vehicle. It should have taken just a moment to decide where to go and how to divide the water between us, but we prolonged the decision — perhaps because planning a day on a stream is another enjoyable part of the experience.

The omens for the day were good. The previous evening, we talked about the joy of maintaining a passion for fly-fishing, even as we grow older. We weren't claiming it as a particularly worthwhile thing, just feeling lucky that we cared about something. It's not just the fishing, either. It has been a rich source of friends at a time when too many finish busy working lives without close friends, and even fewer reasons to get excited about anything.

The relentless winds of October had given way to settled November. The evening was mild and still. I stepped into the dark to make a call home and was captured by the sky. A bright cuticle of moon sat low in the western sky, above a line of silver birches. The crescent of light cast a pale grey glow over the rest of the moon, while bright Venus was suspended directly above. When I look at these dark Southland skies, I'm left feeling on the verge of something beyond understanding and explanation, but with a hope that if I stand here long enough I might learn something of interest about my borrowed existence. Bob and JD joined me to take in the view.

It looked like a night scene by Edward Hopper — a living room glimpsed through the silver birches; the glow of light spilling from the window; a suggestion of an event taking place out of sight; and, above, dark space studded with diamonds. In the foreground an empty road, a fence and three friends staring at the night sky thinking how lucky they were.

We finished our fishing plans over an unhurried breakfast of eggs, bacon, toast and strong coffee. JD was to go in below us to try a section he hadn't fished. Bob and I were to drive through a farm upstream: Bob was to fish the water below the car, and I was to go above.

We found the farmer at the implement shed.

'Morning,' I said. 'We're hoping to go down to the stream to fish, if that's okay.'

He wrapped a worn hand around his lower jaw and looked at me as though he was a doctor contemplating my condition. 'Sure,' he said, 'I'm pleased to see you guys fishing the stream.'

'Thanks,' I said. 'Which is the best way down? Last week I drove down the lane to the left, and then in over the ploughed paddock.'

He rubbed his chin, looked towards our destination and thought for an extended moment. 'That paddock's sown now,' he said. 'Go right at the end of the lane. Head over to that tractor, he said, pointing to a dilapidated tractor on a ridge. If you cut diagonally over the one beyond that you should be fine.'

'One of these days I'll push the lane all the way to the stream, he said. Make it easier for us all.'

Bob listened to the conversation through his open window. 'I can't believe how generous these guys are with access,' he said as we drove over the paddocks to the stream. 'Where else in the world do you find that?'

I left Bob and walked upstream for fifteen minutes, staying clear of the banks. The stream, which had been in flood for much of the past month, was perfect now. Its flow is only about a cumec, and it is a miracle that it hasn't been overwhelmed by the impact of intensive farming on the soils it has deposited on this valley floor for aeons. The stream has survived being treated badly for decades, although I wonder how many lives it has left.

The air smelt of freshly cut grass, cows, sheep and the earthy scent of the water. The stream flowed dark and slow under a grey sky that draped the western hills with misty rain, flecks of white foam tracking its current lines. Willows crowded one bank or the other, but rarely both. I checked my watch and decided I had left Bob enough water. I eased down the grassy bank, slid into the knee-deep flow and waited while the ripples left by my gentle entry decayed. Water bulged softly against the floating strands of grass a few metres above me, betraying a feeding trout, and towards the centre of the stream a widely spaced dorsal and tail fin broke the surface, held for a moment, and then disappeared. In a patch of light a little further upstream, I saw two more fish feeding, one curving onto its side to get a better angle to scoop caddis larvae from the stream bottom. The stream had a huge population of cased caddis, and I was sure that was what the trout would be picking from the stones.

The stream made little noise. Along the long quiet pools there was just the sound of water being pushed against my legs — only where the water tumbled through the rocky seams at the head of the pools did its gentle energy convert to a watery murmur. Beyond the stream I heard the hum of bees gathering pollen from flowering willows.

I tied on one of Bob's snowshoe-hare emergers, even though few trout rose. I felt that a nymph would have caught in the algae and weed in the shallow water. It was an act of faith that the trout would take an emerger in the film. My first cast spooked a couple I hadn't seen in the shadowy water, and they ricocheted up the pool like well-hit billiard balls, scaring others. I murmured a curse and pushed my back into the bank to wait for the melee to settle. Eventually I made a short cast upstream of a feeding trout, the leader touching down in a pleasing pile of curves that would add distance to the drag-free drift. It rose, and because it was close I was able to watch the fly tip gently over its lip. The hooked trout disturbed the other fish in the small pool before I slid it into my net. It was time to move on, although it was difficult to travel upstream without spooking others. I edged forward, stopping every few metres while I scanned for feeding fish. The signs were mostly subtle shifts of the stream's surface: an unnatural bulge, faint ripples heading in an odd direction. Sometimes a fin would show, and once in a while a trout would rise.

It's not always like this, but today the windows of light showed trout in improbable numbers. They cruised slowly, often two or three within a few metres of each other, picking cased caddis from the stony bottom. The parade of fish continued as I edged upstream for the next couple of hours. I followed a trout about thirty metres as it grazed on caddis. Even in water this shallow it took no notice of my emerger suspended in the surface film centimetres from its head. Eventually I got the fly in front of the trout as it lifted its focus from the stony bottom, and sucked in the fly as though that was exactly what it had been looking for. I landed several before I realised I needed to move faster to make my rendezvous.

Close to the car I found four fish rising in a deep slow pool. They hung close to the surface in the open shafts of current that flowed between dense beds of plants, trout, and plants swaying with the current, moving like long grass on a breezy day. I waded waist-deep to within three rod-lengths of them, and landed my fly just upstream of the closest fish, the fly line on top of the plants leaving only my leader on the water. The pectoral fins of the trout stiffened in that moment when a bolt for cover is as likely an outcome as a rise to the fly. On this occasion the trout tilted up and took the fly. It is almost a miracle to land trout in these weed-choked areas, and within a minute my rod was fully bent by both trout and plants. By the time I got it to the net the combination of weed and trout weighed close to eight pounds, with the trout contributing about half the total.

We don't have a tradition in New Zealand of being able to amble through our rural countryside — there are few opportunities to walk away from the road and take the time to observe the fine detail of the land. The chance to sit in the shade of a willow and watch the water, the insects, swallows, terns, ducks and even the odd rat, is lost to most. As I grow older this element of my fly-fishing has become at least as important as catching trout. Casting a fly gives me a chance to see this world, because to fly fish well, you need to find a way to enter this natural place, not loudly at the top of the food chain but quietly somewhere in the middle of it, connected to it by the fly attached to a leader, a fly line and rod. My therapy has become these long rambles through the countryside, spending a day like a Buddhist, mind focused on this single experience. My footprints will remain beside the stream until the next rain, but the imprint left on me by these days walking beside a stream lasts longer. I'm left with a better sense of what can and can't be bought and sold; some understanding of the complex harmony of these places and an altered perspective of where I stand in the scheme of things. I didn't understand that this would be part of the journey when I cycled to the river almost six decades ago, rod in hand, green fishing bag over my shoulder — focused only on catching trout.

SEASONS

The things that have excited me about fishing have changed over the years. When I was a boy, worm-fishing on the Mataura, I was happy to sit in the frosty half-light at the start of the day watching my rod tip. Hoping against hope that I'd see what usually started as nothing more than a tap, but would end with the rod bending over the forked stick that held it tethered to the bank, while the trout ran for freedom. I felt the same excitement on the Waikaka Stream, just a couple of blocks from our house on Wentworth Street, when I fished for eels. I would crouch under the old wooden bridge, holding twine between my thumb and forefinger, waiting for the vibration that told me an eel had started nibbling the smelly meat on my hook. Looking back, I think there was something about the mystery of what lay unseen in the deep holes that grabbed my attention.

When I reached my teens, I started threadline fishing — casting Tobys, Glimmys and articulated trout across the current and winding them back, hoping to attract trout or perch. Once in a while I saw a fish chase the lure before grabbing it and throwing itself into the air as it tried to escape. There was something about seeing a trout chase the lure that captivated me, and besides, fishing the threadline gave me an excuse to explore the banks of the river.

I began fly fishing in the early 1960s. I could have carried on fishing the worm, or casting metal lures. They are productive ways to fish. Early on I was drawn to running water, but that need could have been satisfied without a fly rod. And I didn't need a fly rod to have an excuse to wander through the countryside. All of those things are able to be experienced with a threadline reel and rod. In the end I think I picked up a fly rod because I loved the idea of it, without being able to articulate where the source of the attraction lay.

There was something about the image of fly-fishing that drew me in from the start. Perhaps it was simply that I wanted to look like the men I had seen fly-fishing as I dawdled over the Gore bridge on my way home from the movies. It looked like a grown-up, magical thing to do. And when we camped in the Queenstown campground there was an older fly fisherman with a clipped grey moustache who had a campsite near ours. Most mornings he left early for Moke Lake and almost always returned with a couple of trout. He stood out in the campground because he drove an Armstrong Siddeley, which looked to me like a small version of the Rolls-Royce cars I had seen in magazines, and went off with his fly rod wearing a tweed jacket and woollen cap. I'm pretty sure he had seen me walking down to the lake with my rod, so I imagine he knew I fished, and I often hung about his campsite when he left for the lake, desperate that he might ask me to go along, but he never did. Mum suggested I should ask if he would take me, but I was too shy to talk to him.

The image of the cast was also magnetically attractive. There is grace in the look and feel of a fly line slicing the air. My friend Kevin Ireland, wrote in his most recent poetry collection *Keeping a Grip* about coming towards the end of his fishing days. In *Time on the Waters* he wrote:

Indeed I'd pack it in for good
right now, accept the loss,
hang my rod up on the wall
With my old split canes

if it wasn't for the fact I'd love
another go — feel the looping
tug of the line swooping one last
time across the waters.

There is a strong hunting element involved in fly-fishing. In the mostly clear southern waters, being able to see the trout before they see me is critical. And once spotted, getting close enough to these wild creatures to present a fly with delicacy and accuracy requires the stealth of a cat stalking a mouse. This closeness to the trout adds intimacy to fly-fishing — as does the need to observe the insects, the water and the birds that often offer the first clues as to what's happening in the river. Fly-fishing has opened my eyes to a slice of the natural world that might otherwise have remained a mystery.

Fly-fishing has a timeless quality to it that adds to its allure. While rods and reels have improved over the centuries, the essence of fly-fishing hasn't changed much. It is still all about presenting a fly made of feathers and fur, using a rod, to help propel a weighted line towards a fish. I am confident that if I was lucky enough to travel backwards in time, say to the late sixteenth century, and was invited to fish a chalk stream in England, I could manage with the tackle available then.

Success came slowly when I started. I had no one to teach me how to cast so I flailed away with my rod, trying to remember what the men fishing by the bridge did to get the line carving the air. And even when I managed to get my fly out into the current, I hardly touched a fish. The only thing that kept me going for a year or two was the elevated image I had of fly-fishing.

Once I started catching trout I looked to land as many as I could, irrespective of whether I was taking them on little dry flies, or on heavy nymph imitations deep down where I couldn't see them. For a time I measured my progress by the numbers of trout caught. Almost imperceptibly, though, the things that kept me fly-fishing changed. The visual intimacy involved in seeing the fish became more important than simply catching them. The trajectory of the change wasn't as neat as it appears with the benefit of hindsight, but eventually I became bored with taking unseen fish from the depths.

Salt water fly-fishing also played a role in changing my attitude. The size and power of the fish I hunted in the warm waters of the Florida Keys in the 1990s threatened to derail my interest in trout. Putting a fly the size of something a trout would take in front of a hundred-pound tarpon, or the challenge involved in getting a permit to take a fly, made fishing on my local rivers feel tame.

My true home waters, though, are the trout streams of southern New Zealand, and the streams of the vast Mataura catchment in particular. It is the landscape of my life, and is where many of my connections with the people I care about started. Giving up on it wasn't an option. Eventually I managed to rediscover the magic involved in placing a tiny fly as close as I dared to the face of a wild trout, in the hope I could convince it that my offering of hook and perhaps cotton, deer hair and the fluff from a duck's bum was the real thing. There is an audacity about it that captivates me, and it's all the better because it happens in full view. It is what keeps drawing me back to be with my friends, the rivers — and the trout around which it all revolves.

While it wasn't my intention to write on how to catch trout in the Mataura catchment, I reluctantly decided — because so much has already been written on the subject — to include some material on how I fish the river now. It is a personal view, based on the sort of fishing I have grown to love. Most of the time I fish upstream for trout I can see, using flies that float and nymphs that sink through the surface film. The flies I use are usually small (size 14 and smaller) because the insects I am hoping to roughly represent are themselves tiny. This style of fly-fishing is particularly suited to the creeks, streams and rivers that make up the Mataura system, because of the regular hatches of insects that attract trout into places where they can be seen. There is nothing special about the gear I use. My rods are usually 5 or 6 weight, nine footers. On some of the creeks I sometimes use short 3-weight rods — not because the trout are smaller, because often the opposite is true — but as a way of staying clear of the canopy of vegetation that can overhang them. My treasure is a little cane rod built by Nick Taransky. It is exquisite in the hand, functions perfectly, and lifts my heart when I dare to take it out. My monofilament leaders are mostly between nine and twelve feet long, and the tippets I use break at five or six pounds.

I use a small number of unremarkable flies. They include bead-head nymphs, the most common being a size 16, sparsely tied in dark mahogany material; a no-hackle dun with an upright wing of deer hair and CDC body, tied on a size 16–18 hook, a para-dun with pink post for ease of seeing, again in size 16; a mayfly emerger (Bob Wyatt has these covered in his fine books on fly selection); Royal Wulff dry flies to cover most of the beetle patterns I need; and some tiny willow-grub flies. I usually fish with one fly, but once in a while will fish two at a time, and then mostly to allow me to manipulate the depth of the fly. There is nothing magical or secret about the flies, but they do the business for me. As Bob Wyatt says, it's not what you got, it's how you use it that matters.

The sort of fishing I enjoy is like the stalking of a wild creature. To do it well requires the angler to get close to the trout without being seen or heard, before presenting the fly in a way that gives the fish no cause for alarm.

To fish well, be careful of your footfall, both in and out of the water. Be a gentle wader. Wear clothes that blend into the background, and use banks and vegetation to obscure your profile. Stay low and move slowly when close to the fish.

Good anglers learn to really see what is going on in, and around, the water. Watch the terns, swallows and gulls, because they often give the first hint of what is happening to the insects of the river. Learn about the life cycle of the insects the trout feed on — the deleatidium, and various caddis flies in particular — because the timing of their life cycles drives the feeding behaviour of trout. Turn over stones on the riverbed, because the insects crawling on them act as a guide to the health of the stream, and can indicate what the trout will be looking for.

Time spent on the water is the best way to learn where trout will be at different times of the day, and during different hatches. Learn also to read the water; to see the slightest blemish on the surface caused by a trout interfering with the flow, and learn to piece together the fragments of shadow and movement that betray trout riding the current, because only rarely do they present themselves in full view.

Most importantly perhaps — learn to cast. To catch trout in the Mataura, or anywhere wild trout inhabit, requires the angler to, as often as possible, present the fly with precision. To do that, and allow the fly to drift as naturally as possible towards the trout requires considerable skill. They are the skills possessed by the tiny proportion of anglers who catch most of the fish. The angler should be able to cast in ways that curve the fly to the right, or to the left, and to make casts that impart a series of snake-like curves into line and leader. This can be done by emulating others who do it well, by reading how to do it, by spending time on the water to learn — or, best of all, by finding a qualified instructor and paying them to impart the skills required.

What follows is a group of seasonal stories, set around the theme of the sort of fly-fishing that keeps pulling me back to the river.

SPRING

Most years I can leapfrog from one hatch to another on the Mataura. Mayflies bookend the season. They can be found from the first day of the season, hatching on the rain-fed tributaries, often on days when showers fall from gale-pushed clouds and the water is slowly warmed by shafts of spring sunshine. I have watched these hatches for decades, and while I know that temperature and humidity play a part in triggering them, the real alchemy involved in the process of the hatch remains a mystery. That they don't happen with precision adds to their allure.

Mayflies define dry-fly-fishing on the Mataura for me. I am enchanted by their ephemeral beauty and the complexity of their life cycle — the transformation they make from an insect that crawls prosaically over the stony bottom of the river, to one that takes to the sky on wings as delicate as a spider's web. What matters to the dry-fly angler, though, is the few metres they drift, like tiny yachts erecting their sails on the broken surface of the river; that brief moment when the trout take them, before the survivors climb into the air and take their chances with the terns, gulls and swallows.

By the middle of spring the hatches have usually developed on the main stems of the Mataura and Waikaia, even when they carry the blue-grey remnants of late melting snow. A few years back, when Kevin was down for his spring visit to Balfour, the Mataura was in just such a state — rushing past, high, cold and grey. On his last day we cast at big trout in a backwater some distance from the river. While walking to the car in the late afternoon I looked back towards the Mataura, my attention caught by gulls and terns flying in a wheeling mass, as they do when plucking mayflies from the air. I returned the next day and sat by the bank looking at the water racing by, and waited. About two-thirty, some gulls took off and a smattering of duns bounced along on the ripply water. Within fifteen minutes flurries of duns were climbing into the cool air, and the gulls had been joined by swallows and terns. Trout were stacked at the top of the ripple, at least a dozen of them, their backs only just covered by the water that carried flies to them. I tied on a little emerger and, because the fish were so preoccupied by the density of the hatch, I was able to get within a couple of rod lengths of them. I hooked the rear fish first, pulling it back into the pool to leave the others undisturbed, and proceeded to land eight or nine in the next hour, stopping only when a jet boat pulled up below me and two men stood and watched as I landed the last couple. I didn't want to make it look easy, nor give away just how extraordinary had been the hatch, so I gave up and walked over to talk with them. Turned out they were doing survey work for Environment Southland and weren't fishermen, so I needn't have worried.

SUMMER

Around thirty years earlier I encountered mayfly spinners just a few hundred metres upstream of the scene just described. It was before I owned a place in Balfour. Randy, Jim and I drove west one Friday night in early December. We pitched a couple of tents by the edge of the river and fished without much success for trout slashing at adult caddis hatching in the dark. By eleven we were drinking gin and tonic, and debating how to determine the difference between a moth and an adult caddis.

'It's the scales on their wings that give them away. Moths

have them, and caddis don't,' I said, as a combination of moths and caddis flew around our gas lamp. 'Grab one and see,' I suggested.

'You're right,' said Randy, but Jim remained unconvinced. The quality of the conversation and the amount of gin consumed proved to be negatively correlated, and soon after midnight I climbed into my sleeping bag and fell asleep.

I woke early to the hard reality of the morning — the bed of stones pushed into my back, and my mouth was rough and dry. In the half-light I saw hundreds of moths and caddis still clinging to the tent roof. I crawled the few metres to the edge of the river, gulped from the flow and splashed handfuls of water over my head. With my eyes almost at water level I looked upstream. A few metres above me a trout pushed its nose through the flat surface, and while my brain slowly processed what was going on, a mayfly spinner, wings splayed on the surface of the river, floated past. I crawled back to my tent, grabbed a rod and tied on a spent spinner imitation. I poked my head into the tent. 'Randy, get up. There's a rise on.'

'Bullshit,' was all I got so I left him and, still on my knees, flipped a low-angled cast above the closest trout. Around the time I landed my fifth I yelled again in the direction of the tent, 'They're still going! Get out here!' Randy pushed his big frame out of the tent flap, his sceptical eyes blinking in the light. When he saw the rising trout above me he scrambled for his rod and started fishing. We landed a few more before the sun came up and the drift of spinners slowed.

By the time Jim woke the big fish had gone, leaving just a few tiddlers making splashy rises. Mid-morning we decided that we didn't have the energy to carry on into the heat of the day so made our way back to Dunedin, the lively conversation of the previous evening gone.

***

The end of the early-season mayfly hatches overlaps the emergence of a variety of other insects that keep trout focused on the surface of the river. When the evenings warm in late spring, brown beetles bumble their way onto the water, and by December brilliantly coloured mānuka beetles can be found in the bushy sections of the upper river.

Some days in early summer riffle beetles, the size of a few pinheads, drift beside grassy banks to be taken by trout with the gentlest of rises, leaving a disturbance as faint as a rain-drop on the surface glaze. And by mid-summer trout take blowflies and cicadas with gusto.

Caddis flies hatch on settled summer evenings, and trout torpedo them as they run and flutter across the flow. In the past I've fished the caddis into the dark. It's best done on moonless nights, when I cast at the sounds of splashy rises and set the hook by feel. It has been a few years since I've fished a caddis hatch, because these days we are more likely to be engaged in conversation about all manner of things in Balfour than standing in the pitch dark, thigh-deep in the river.

Though I have fished the river with a fly rod for much of my life, I am still confounded once in a while by what brings trout up to feed at the surface. In the past year I had just such an experience when I found them rising and had no idea what was going on until the day ended. It was in the Nokomai Gorge, on a warm day in early December. No vehicles had beaten me to the gate at the end of the road. At Randy's Ripple I landed a couple of fish that took a para-dun, and then another from a shallow glide a hundred metres further on. I ate my lunch while being warmed by the sun in this valley that I have known since the 1970s. It lifts my heart still just to be there, let alone fish for the solid trout. It is the start of the high country — the bush-clad lower slopes and steep tussock-softened ridge-lines foreshadowing the mountainous birth of the Mataura, seventy kilometres to the north-west.

Soon after my break I came to a deep pool where the river was deflected from the eastern bank by a rock face. Five trout levitated under a line of foam that snaked its way over the pale turquoise water, their snouts sending off ripples as they carved through the surface to feed. No swallows or terns took insects from the air, and I couldn't see any upright wings in the flow so I doubted they were rising to mayfly duns. In my uncertainty I persisted with a size 16 para-dun and threw a long cast towards the fish at the rear of the group. It took on the first drift, but the fly didn't stick so I allowed it to settle before hooking and landing the trout on the next cast. As though there was something magical going on, the remaining four fish all took the fly.

No trout rose in the next few hundred metres where the river bounced downstream through a couple of often-productive ripples, but in the pool above I found several rising. For the next couple of hours I hurried past the fast water, looking instead for the deep slow pools where the fish fed. By late afternoon I had hooked most of the fish encountered, and landed fifteen. I became so engrossed with the fishing that I lost track of time. My focus narrowed to nothing more than the fish, the place I needed to land the fly, and the eddies of current between fish and fly that might upset their perfect conjunction. I killed one to take home, but instead of immediately gutting it to check its stomach contents I placed it in shade and hurried back to the water.

By the time I stopped I had landed eighteen in the afternoon, and twenty-one for the day. Several were over four pounds, and only three less than a couple. That is as good as fly-fishing for trout gets — anywhere. Thirty looked possible, but I'd told Sue I would head home to Dunedin rather than stay on in Balfour, so I collected the fish I had left from under the overhang of grass and, with trout still rising, began the hour-long walk back to the car. Partway back I stopped to look closely at the river to see if I could find a clue as to what the trout were feeding on. A couple of horn-cased caddis swirled about on the surface of an eddy at the edge of a glide. I scooped them into the palm of my hand and wondered if they were what had attracted the trout. No nymph shucks or spent mayfly spinners floated at the quiet edge of the water, suggesting they weren't responsible for the rising trout.

Back at my Jeep I sliced open the belly of the fish and found that its stomach was packed with horn-cased caddis. I had previously experienced caddis larvae drifting in the surface film on the Waimea Stream, but this was a first for me on the Mataura.

***

About the middle of a warm breezy day, a week or two before Christmas, I often see a change in the way trout feed. They start tucking themselves close into lines of willows, holding near the surface where they rise with metronomic regularity to take willow grubs falling to the river. The fall of the willow grub marks the beginning of the most challenging, interesting and at times frustrating dry-fly-fishing of the season. Mostly I enjoy the challenge, but once in a while they drive me nuts. Presentation on the mostly slick surface in and around willows can be a challenge, but I sense that something else contributes to making these trout hard to catch.

I suspect part of the problem lies with the enormous number of grubs on offer. They are transported to the trout on the current, as though being dropped onto a conveyor belt. It is easy feeding for the fish which can mostly hold their station and, with the slightest of tilts, let the grubs drop into their mouths. The only downside for the fish is that the grubs are tiny, so they must take hundreds every day to sustain themselves. I suspect it's the regularity of the taking that makes the trout picky. This is the closest I've come to admitting the possibility that trout might be selective about the flies anglers use. I'm a supporter of the theory put forward by my friend and angling writer Bob Wyatt, whose view is that if you get the presentation right, a general impression of the insect being imitated is all that is required to get the job done. The willow grub is an absurdly easy insect to imitate, and for a number of years I believed the pattern I use had been good enough, and the reason for the refusals lay with my poor presentation of the fly.

During the season just past I had a number of days fishing for trout taking willow grubs. The early results were as they had been for the last decade or so: an unreasonable number of refusals. There was a lucky randomness about the success I had which offended my sense of perfection.

Some afternoons, when the warm wind dislodged thousands of willow grubs, I gave up fishing and clambered out onto willow branches to get as close to the rising trout as I could — close enough to see the grubs hit the water. For a short time the tiny dints they made on the surface showed as silver dots. The trout were particularly focused on the newly dropped grubs and took almost every one that drifted past, even if they had to swing a metre across the current to grab them. They managed the feat on both slick and broken water.

My attention went back to the imitation I was using. When I dropped a few of my flies into a palm full of real grubs, the artificial ones looked convincing enough in every way — apart from size. The real grubs were half the size of my flies. Back in Balfour I tied a new batch on the tiniest hooks I could find. They looked closer to the size of the real grubs.

Over the following weeks I put the fly to the test. The weather was hot and the river shrivelled by drought, but enough trout fed on the grubs to allow me to test the new flies. For the first few days the results were as I hoped. Fewer fish refused the fly than had been my recent experience, and I regularly hooked seven or eight in an afternoon, although a number dropped off before they were landed because the tiny hooks proved hard to set. It was perhaps close to a fifty per cent improvement on my earlier efforts, although the fall of grubs was halted by cooling weather before I was confident that I had found an enduring solution.

AUTUMN

Summer usually begins its retreat sometime in March. Nights cool, a frost or two settles on the ground and the days contract. This is about the time I put on my waders to keep the chill of the river from my legs. Most autumns the weather is settled. Skeins of mallards crisscross the sky to and from the paddocks of stubble and remnant grain which fatten them for the approaching winter. The willow grubs are gone, as are most of the terrestrial insects that have attracted trout to the surface during summer.

My mood changes with the season. I am conflicted by a love of the sharper light that comes with autumn and the bleaching of summer's exuberance from the landscape, but there is something about the yellowing of the leaves and dying of the thistles — along with a myriad of other things — that leaves me feeling melancholic. Too many reminders that all things must pass. Someone whom I once loved suggested it was simply that I hated the end of the fishing season, and there might be truth in that also.

The trout, too, feel the imperative of the changing season, feeding hard to build their reserves for the rigours of spawning, just two or three months away. Their colours change as though a painter has been at work. Olive backs darken, haloed spots become more pronounced, and a yellow hue, the colour of aged willow leaves, often develops on their lower flanks from the operculum to the tail. The spawning females begin to bulge with eggs, and the kypes on the males extend and contort.

The cooling water compresses the hatch of mayfly duns which at their most concentrated can, when seen in the sharp, low-angled light, look like a charcoal-coloured blizzard. By late autumn they often don't break the surface until 1.30 p.m., and if the day is cold the hatch might be over by three-thirty or four.

In the autumn I usually arrive at the river a couple of hours before the hatch is due. While I sometimes prospect the water with a nymph, mostly I am content to get into position and wait on the hatch to begin. It is rare for me to see many trout during this time of waiting, but around an hour before the hatch begins, they make their move, working their way out of the deep holes into the runs where the nymphs live on the stony bottom. Swallows and terns make the odd prospective flight over the water, their sharp eyes looking for the first of the duns. The start of the hatch is usually marked by a swallow making a sharp lifting turn as it takes a fly, or by ripples pushing outwards from the snout of a trout taking an emerging dun in the surface film.

For an hour or two I fish as though in a trance, with my focus on rise forms or the shadowy outline of the trout as they harvest the duns from the surface. I've fished for these rising trout for so long it has become an instinctive thing. I change my fly from emerger to dun based on signals that are so subtle that I'm not sure I can describe them with honesty. On the best of days, often south of Mataura township, I am able to cast at rising fish for a couple of hours without moving more than a hundred metres.

Late in the hatch I often find mayfly spinners returning to the water to lay their eggs on the slick flow above the ripples. Once the spinners have deposited their eggs they go where the currents take them. Eventually their wings fall flat to the surface and, like dead willow leaves, end up drifting in quiet eddies close to the bank. Because the spinners aren't going anywhere, the trout take them slowly, as though they have all day to do it. The languid takes, usually on chrome-flat surfaces, make taking these trout a serious challenge because every flaw in the presentation of the fly is obvious.

One of my favourite memories of late-season spinner falls goes back a few decades, when the opening of the duck-shooting season overlapped with the end of trout fishing. That day, the gauze-like wings of the spent spinners threw off minuscule flashes of light from the low sun while trout mooched along the shallows, tail and dorsal fins cutting through the surface as they sipped the spinners, accompanied by the thud of shotguns firing at ducks that wheeled into the pale sky. I stayed by the river while the sun threw its last rays across the almost naked willow trees. Trout rose into the dusk, and I didn't want to leave. It was the last weekend of the season, and I wasn't sure I could face up to being away from the river for five months.